Simply Stravinsky

Simply Stravinsky

PIETER VAN DEN TOORN

SIMPLY CHARLY
NEW YORK

Copyright © 2020 by Pieter van den Toorn

Cover Illustration by Vladymyr Lukash
Cover Design by Scarlett Rugers

All rights reserved. No part of this publication may be reproduced, distributed, or transmitted in any form or by any means, including photocopying, recording, or other electronic or mechanical methods, without the prior written permission of the publisher, except in the case of brief quotations embodied in critical reviews and certain other noncommercial uses permitted by copyright law. For permission requests, write to the publisher at the address below.

permissions@simplycharly.com

ISBN: 978-1-943657-32-2

Brought to you by http://simplycharly.com

Contents

Praise for *Simply Stravinsky*	vii
Other *Great Lives*	ix
Series Editor's Foreword	x
Preface	xi
Acknowledgments	xiii
Introduction	1
1. Years of Apprenticeship	11
2. To *The Firebird* (1910)	21
3. *Petrushka* (1911)	35
4. *The Rite of Spring* (1913)	47
5. The Swiss Years (I); *The Wedding* (Les Noces) (1917-23)	60
6. The Swiss Years (II): *Renard* (1916)	76
7. The Swiss Years (III): *The Soldier's Tale* (1918)	82
8. Stravinsky the Rhythmic Genius	89
9. Performance Practice and Aesthetic Belief	98
10. Neoclassicism Born	106
11. Neoclassicism (I); Early Years	114
12. Neoclassicism (II): High Watermarks	126
13. Neoclassicism (III): Late Years	139
14. The Serial Period	149
15. Stravinsky's Legacy	165
Endnotes	169

Suggested Reading	174
About the Author	176
A Word from the Publisher	177

Praise for *Simply Stravinsky*

"This is a short book but a teeming one, boiling over with the insights that have accrued over forty years and more, ever since Pieter van den Toorn set the musicological world on its ear with his revelations about Stravinsky's creative methods, deduced from an unprecedentedly close and fruitful examination of the published scores. Since then he has been at the manuscripts as well, and has made even further-reaching observations about Stravinsky's epochal rhythmic innovations. All of this he now places at the disposal of musicians and general readers, laid out with a chronology of the composer's life and times—a great gift to us all and a fitting crown to a most distinguished scholarly career."
　–**Richard Taruskin, author of *Stravinsky and the Russian Traditions***

"Pieter van den Toorn brings fresh insights to the life and work of one of the twentieth century's most written-about composers. He has devoted his entire career to examining how Stravinsky's music 'works' and now shares that deep understanding with a wide readership. The great strength of this book is the way it tells the life through the music, eschewing much of the quotidian tittle-tattle to focus on the essentials of the music's harmonic and rhythmic organization. It certainly made me return to familiar music with new ears."
　–**Jonathan Cross, Professor of Musicology, University of Oxford**

"A readable and comprehensible study by one of our leading Stravinsky theorists. Pieter van den Toorn has the gift of guiding the reader gently and agreeably through some quite intricate matters while painting a lucid overall picture."

—Stephen Walsh, author of *Stravinsky: A Creative Spring: Russia and France, 1882-1934*

"Pieter is among the foremost Stravinsky scholars in the world. His new book *Simply Stravinsky* is a synthesis of musical analysis, history, and criticism. What is remarkable about this book is that it presents a sophisticated account of Stravinsky's musical achievements accessible to a broad audience. And even more impressive is that it not only provides readers with a stimulating account of Stravinsky's works within their rich intellectual and cultural context, but also opens their ears to the joy and wonders of the music itself."

—David Bernstein, Professor of Music, Mills College

"Stravinsky was both grounded in tradition and a breaker of tradition, and Pieter van den Toorn's insightful book shows us both sides of him. There's a great deal to learn here of Stravinsky's methods of composition, which remained consistent in spite of the radical changes of direction and style throughout his career, which are explained in fascinating detail. It's no wonder that Stravinsky is so many composers' favorite composer!"

—Colin Matthews, English composer and Prince Consort Professor of Music and Fellow of the Royal College of Music

Other *Great Lives*

Simply Austen by Joan Klingel Ray
Simply Beckett by Katherine Weiss
Simply Beethoven by Leon Plantinga
Simply Chekhov by Carol Apollonio
Simply Chomsky by Raphael Salkie
Simply Chopin by William Smialek
Simply Darwin by Michael Ruse
Simply Descartes by Kurt Smith
Simply Dickens by Paul Schlicke
Simply Dirac by Helge Kragh
Simply Einstein by Jimena Canales
Simply Eliot by Joseph Maddrey
Simply Euler by Robert E. Bradley
Simply Faulkner by Philip Weinstein
Simply Fitzgerald by Kim Moreland
Simply Freud by Stephen Frosh
Simply Gödel by Richard Tieszen
Simply Hegel by Robert L. Wicks
Simply Hitchcock by David Sterritt
Simply Joyce by Margot Norris
Simply Machiavelli by Robert Fredona
Simply Napoleon by J. David Markham & Matthew Zarzeczny
Simply Nietzsche by Peter Kail
Simply Proust by Jack Jordan
Simply Riemann by Jeremy Gray
Simply Sartre by David Detmer
Simply Tolstoy by Donna Tussing Orwin
Simply Turing by Michael Olinick
Simply Wagner by Thomas S. Grey
Simply Wittgenstein by James C. Klagge

Series Editor's Foreword

Simply Charly's "Great Lives" series offers brief but authoritative introductions to the world's most influential people–scientists, artists, writers, economists, and other historical figures whose contributions have had a meaningful and enduring impact on our society.

Each book provides an illuminating look at the works, ideas, personal lives, and the legacies these individuals left behind, also shedding light on the thought processes, specific events, and experiences that led these remarkable people to their groundbreaking discoveries or other achievements. Additionally, every volume explores various challenges they had to face and overcome to make history in their respective fields, as well as the little-known character traits, quirks, strengths, and frailties, myths, and controversies that sometimes surrounded these personalities.

Our authors are prominent scholars and other top experts who have dedicated their careers to exploring each facet of their subjects' work and personal lives.

Unlike many other works that are merely descriptions of the major milestones in a person's life, the "Great Lives" series goes above and beyond the standard format and content. It brings substance, depth, and clarity to the sometimes-complex lives and works of history's most powerful and influential people.

We hope that by exploring this series, readers will not only gain new knowledge and understanding of what drove these geniuses, but also find inspiration for their own lives. Isn't this what a great book is supposed to do?

Charles Carlini, Simply Charly
New York City

Preface

Igor Stravinsky never lacked for an appreciative audience. The international celebrity that was his with *The Firebird* in 1910 was his late in life as well. His neoclassical works of the 1920s, 30s, and 40s, although less popular than the ballet scores composed earlier for the Ballets Russes, attracted a devoted following. Constantly on the move during this period, introducing his music in Europe and the United States, he conducted and performed at the piano.

The serial and 12-tone works of his American years (1939 until his death in 1971) were not popular at all, but Stravinsky was always careful to cushion the new with the old and the familiar in his programs. In 1959, he began co-authoring books of comment and reminiscence with Robert Craft, his associate who, when not assisting him at the podium, began publishing his own studies of the composer. These publications attracted a wide audience, and for a while, the two were very much in the limelight. In celebration of Stravinsky's 80th birthday in 1962, President John Kennedy and his wife, Jacqueline, held a dinner in his honor at the White House.

Simply Stravinsky takes a fresh look at these events and circumstances, at the composer and his legacy, as well as the music and the biography that surrounds it. It reexamines the conditions attending the conception of many of Stravinsky's works, the years of apprenticeship in St. Petersburg, the collaboration with Sergei Diaghilev and the Ballets Russes, the neoclassical years in France, and the serial ones in California. Above all, it explores the rhythmic, melodic, and harmonic qualities of Stravinsky's music as they relate to his aesthetic ideals and the strict performing style he championed as a conductor and pianist.

In all these matters, the book is intended for the general reader with, ideally, a modest background in music and a listening experience of perhaps two or three Stravinsky works. The text was conceived as an introduction—in other words, to give the reader/

listener a broad view of the composer's world. Stimulating some further interest in the music of this extraordinary composer was its ultimate objective.

Pieter van den Toorn
Santa Barbara, CA

Acknowledgments

I am grateful to the Paul Sacher Foundation in Basel, Switzerland, for its permission, extended some years ago, to examine first-hand swaths of the Stravinsky Archive. Included in this material were musical sketches and drafts, as well as old programs, reviews, and personal correspondence. Of no less consequence were the six books of interviews and "conversation" authored jointly by the composer and Robert Craft (mostly by Craft, it appears), followed by Craft's own diaries and biographical sketches of the composer. The wealth of information in these volumes about Stravinsky's schedules, habits, and musical inclinations proved invaluable.

Next in line are the recollections of other friends and colleagues of the composer, including, in chronological order, those by C.F. Ramuz (1929), Nicolas Nabokov (1949), Paul Horgan (1972), and, most recently, Mario Bois (1998). Of the many articles and full-scale biographies, those by Richard Taruskin (1996), Stephen Walsh (1999, 2006), Jonathan Cross (2015), and H. Colin Slim (2019) merit citation here.

Of course, the perspective pursued in *Simply Stravinsky* is very much its own, which is especially the case where the discussion of Stravinsky's music is concerned. The musical illustrations were set with great skill by Andre Mount, while Cattarina van den Toorn devoted countless hours to the technical challenges of the project. The staff at the music libraries at the University of California at Santa Barbara and Berkeley were invariably helpful in their advice. And many odds and ends were attended to by Anna-Marie, Linnea, Hendrik, John Willem, and Pieter. I am grateful to them as well.

Introduction

At the time of Stravinsky's death on April 6, 1971, at the age of 88, the speculation among critics centered quite naturally on his legacy. Would his music survive into the next century and perhaps well beyond that? Looking back, what had been the substance and scale of his influence? Had he been, perhaps, in Western art music, the last of the "great composers"?

Stravinsky was certainly the most celebrated composer of the 20th century and possibly the greatest as well, if by "greatest" we mean "deepest," as in the *depth* of the feelings or emotions stirred by his music. Fame arrived early with the three ballets—*The Firebird* (1910), *Petrushka* (1911), and *The Rite of Spring* (1913). The popular success of these ballet scores, overshadowing that of all other classical music of the past century, brought the composer international stardom at the age of 28. And this early success has proved lasting: to this day, the early ballets, along with other Stravinsky music, is performed in concert halls, opera houses, and ballet theaters the world over. Stravinsky and his music are still in vogue, in other words, still very much a part of the contemporary scene.

At the same time, the twists and turns of his creative path were impulsive and contradictory. To many critics and listeners at the time, they seemed incomprehensible. While the stereotypical three-part division may readily be inferred from his music, the radical nature of the changes accompanying the three divisions or "stylistic periods" was unprecedented. Each of the three periods—Russian, neoclassical, and serial—seemed to negate (and even to betray) the one that preceded or succeeded it. Stravinsky's neoclassicism of the 1920s, 30s, and 40s seemed a disavowal of the earlier folkloristic idioms, while serialism seemed a contradiction of his neoclassical ideals.

Consider, by way of comparison, the nearly seamless way in which the three stylistic periods follow each other in Ludwig van Beethoven's music. (Recent scholars have partitioned Beethoven's music in still more sophisticated ways, but the three-part division works well enough for our purposes). An early assimilation of the formal and more technical elements of the Classical style is followed by a gradual *individualization* of those elements—in effect, the arrival of the composer's second, middle, or "heroic" period. This is the Beethoven sound with which audiences are most familiar and, symphony-wise, it begins with the length and drama of the "Eroica" Symphony and ends with the Seventh and Eighth Symphonies.

The distinguishing marks of Beethoven's "late style" include the many theme-and-variation movements that are found in the Ninth Symphony, in the piano sonatas, and string quartets of this era. Extended fugues may also be found in this music, reflective of a renewed interest in the contrapuntal techniques of Johann Sebastian Bach's keyboard music. And Beethoven's sonata forms are now often subject to sudden breaks in tempo and texture. The critic-philosopher Theodor Adorno professed to detect an air of "resignation" in these works, a retreat from the heroics of Beethoven's second period. To follow Adorno's quasi-Marxist critique, feelings of at-oneness with the outside world were followed "catastrophically" by disillusionment and alienation.

But the larger point here is that, regardless of the modifications from one creative stage to the next, the bulk of Beethoven's music *extends* the Classical style that this composer had inherited from his immediate predecessors, including Joseph Haydn and Wolfgang Amadeus Mozart. And the musical language cloaked by that style was shared not only by Beethoven's contemporaries, but also by composers of the Baroque and Romantic eras. Thus, the period extending from about 1650 to the close of the 19th century has long been known musically as the "common practice period." Consisting harmonically of triads derived from the major and minor scales of the diatonic set, this "practice" is hierarchical in nature. The triads gravitate around a central or "tonic" triad. They depart from and return to that triad, acquiring their specific functions in the process, and emitting a sense of motion or *harmonic progression*. On a linear or melodic scale, the connections between triads are lines or parts that follow voice-leading rules, the most important of which is *smoothness*. The triads of a given scale and the functions associated with them form a *key*, and transpositions between keys are called *modulations*.

Tonality is the term usually reserved for these musical processes. The system allowed for a certain structural depth in pitch relationships, one that proved capable of renewing itself or "advancing" through many changing forms, instrumentations, and styles. The art music of the West was bound in this fashion for centuries, as was that of Russia.

Thus, Stravinsky's apprenticeship in St. Petersburg began with piano instruction and very traditional lessons in tonal harmony and counterpoint. The latter were capped by nearly three years (1905-08) of private lessons in composition and orchestration with Nikolai Rimsky-Korsakov. Acquired by such means was a close familiarity with tonal practice and a mastery of instrumentation and the orchestra; an intimate knowledge of 1) Russian folk songs harmonized in a kind of Westernized, tonal fashion (such songs were modal, as a rule), and 2) sequences built on symmetrical scales such as the whole-tone and the octatonic. These skills were brought to fruition with *The Firebird* and the sensational success of its first performance in Paris on June 25, 1910.

However, *The Firebird* was followed in short order by *Petrushka* (1911) and *The Rite of Spring* (1913), two works of truly startling originality. In particular, *The Rite*, with its rhythmic irregularities and sustained dissonances, can seem light-years from the immediately inherited traditions that underlie *The Firebird*.

Changing musical styles and tastes

Exiled in Switzerland during World War I, the composer partly turned his back on this early phase of his creative life. In place of the orchestra, he began composing for small chamber ensembles, and then eventually for singers and groups that resembled peasant bands and the instrumentations of street music. He began cultivating a musical folk language of his own, derived from bits and pieces of authentic Russian folk songs and popular verse. These efforts culminated in *Renard* (1916), *The Wedding* (1917-23), and *The Soldier's Tale* (1918). The period in question, stretching from the composer's years of tutelage in St. Petersburg to *The Wedding*, is often referred to as his *Russian* period.

Returning to France after the war, Stravinsky turned his back once again, this time on the folk languages with which he had worked with such abandon in Switzerland. Starting already with the ballet *Pulcinella* (1920), he began seeking an accommodation with the tonal forms, methods, and styles of the Classical and Baroque eras. This second or middle period is often called *neoclassical*, and it includes works such as the *Octet* (1923), the *Symphony of Psalms* (1930) and, later, the Symphony in C (1940), and the *Symphony in Three Movements* (1945), by which time Stravinsky had moved from France to Los Angeles. A climactic moment in neoclassicism was reached with the composer's collaboration with the poet W. H. Auden on *The Rake's Progress* (1948-51), the opera for which Auden, with the help of Chester Kallman, wrote the libretto.

No doubt, Stravinsky remained true to himself through these neoclassical excursions. From the time of *The Firebird* to *The Rake's Progress*, there were features of pitch, meter, rhythm, and form that prevailed in one way or another, remaining a permanent part of the composer's "voice." And such was the case with many of the serial works as well, especially the early ones composed during the 1950s. Stravinsky was slow and deliberate in his adoption of serial methods. Encouraged by Robert Craft, the conductor and writer who in later years became his close associate and spokesman, Stravinsky began with the study of several scores by Arnold Schoenberg and Anton Webern. The middle part of *In Memoriam Dylan Thomas* (1954) is built on a chromatic series of five notes, while the rows in some of the miniatures of the ballet *Agon* (1953-57) are hexachordal, composed of six successive notes. (As a general rule, all notes of a row are sounded in order before there is a return to the point of departure. A series may be transposed as well as inverted or retrograded–sounded in reverse.)

The "Surge, aquilo" section of *Canticum Sacrum* (1955) was Stravinsky's first completely 12-tone music, and it was followed by six full-scale works, all 12-tone in conception. Many of these latter accompanied religious texts, often biblical or liturgical in origin; their spirit is starkly devotional. As with Beethoven's late works, Stravinsky's feature contrapuntal techniques, in his case, canonic. Along with these full-scale works were seven smaller ones, often short memorials for friends and collaborators who had passed away.

To the extent that the term *style* (as in "stylistic period") implies a musical surface of some kind, inflection at a musical foreground, the term can hardly stand as a descriptive cover for the three giant leaps in musical orientation surveyed briefly above: Russian, neoclassical, and serial. The foundation of Stravinsky's music changed dramatically in each case. The Russian folk songs, tales, and verses of his Swiss years were replaced by the Baroque and Classical models of neoclassicism, and then, during the serial period, by a method of composition even more radically distant from the routines of neoclassicism than the latter were from those of the Russian era.

Somewhat analogous to these dislocations in Stravinsky's creative path were those in the art of Pablo Picasso, a friend of the composer's during the 1910s and 20s in France. (Picasso provided the scenery for the first staged performance of *Pulcinella*, and collaborated with the composer on other occasions as well.) With a good deal of overlapping, Picasso's early "blue" period was followed by cubism until about 1925. A neoclassical phase during the 1920s coincided with Stravinsky's early on; it was followed by surrealism and, toward the end of the 1930s, expressionism.

Yet the concept of *style* might work where the composer's individual voice is concerned, with features that, as we have noted, remained characteristic of Stravinsky's music through much of his career. These features include the following:

1. *Octatonic* harmony, materials that imply, or may originally have been derived from, the octatonic scale (the "diminished scale," as it has long been known in American jazz circles);
2. *Superimpositions* of triads and other forms of vocabulary (placing one triad on top of another, often octatonically related, as a means of creating new dissonant sonorities).
3. *Stratifications* or polyrhythmic textures in which there is a superimposition of motives and chords that repeat according to varying spans or periods;
4. *Ostinatos*, often conceived as separate layers within a stratification;
5. *Block structures* in which two or more heterogeneous and relatively self-contained blocks of material are placed in a kind of abrupt juxtaposition with one another;
6. *Displacements* of repeated themes, motives, or chords relative to the meter (such displacement being so entirely characteristic of Stravinsky's music as to assume the earmarks of a stylistic common denominator);
7. A *strict performance style*, according to which, in the performance of much of Stravinsky's music, the beat is maintained strictly with a minimum of nuance or *rubato*;
8. A *percussive* approach to composition and instrumentation; staccato doublings of legato lines; a percussive use of the piano and string pizzicato as a means of punctuation.

These eight features are *style characteristics* to the extent that they are heard and understood as interacting with one another. One such characteristic can presuppose another. Thus, if the metrical displacement (6) of a repeated motive or melody is to be felt by the listener, then the beat must be maintained evenly (7). And so forth.

Finally, at the time of Stravinsky's arrival on the international scene with *The Firebird* in 1910, the certainties of tonality, of an inherited and shared musical grammar and syntax, were being challenged and even overturned by composers in France and Germany. They were being challenged in Russia as well, if we count the many octatonic or minor-third related sequences in Rimsky-Korsakov's operas and symphonic poems as non-tonal, subject to forces that were symmetrical rather than tonal. The chromaticism of the Prelude to Wagner's *Tristan und Isolde* (1862) is usually cited in connection with the breakdown of tonality, but larger forces, including the drive for originality, were active in sowing the seeds of tonality's exhaustion earlier in the 19th century.

In France, Claude Debussy's music was often triadic and diatonic but no longer tonal, while in Vienna and Germany, Schoenberg's music and that of his students Webern and Alban Berg was "atonal" or serial, founded on the total chromatic; dissonance and the pitch world generally were "emancipated" from tonality. Stravinsky was thus one of many composers reacting to a musical meltdown. Like him, Bela Bartok and Leos Janacek explored the use of authentic folk songs (Hungarian and Moldavian, respectively) in contemporary settings. Sergei Prokofiev and many others cultivated neoclassical idioms that were at times closely related to Stravinsky's.

And so, the dramatic turns of Stravinsky's three stylistic periods were to some extent a reflection of the musical times. This was especially the case with his belated embrace of serialism during the 1950s, methods of composition from which he had sought to distance himself in earlier decades.

On the matter of Stravinsky's "greatness" as a composer, attributions of this kind were once applied freely to contemporary composers. They implied unfathomable depths (or heights) on the part of the music of a given composer, depths that were presumed to be felt widely by a listening public. There was something like a canon; in other words, a consensus to greatness.

However, with the fall of tonality and the disappearance of a musical mainstream in the generations following Stravinsky's, "greatness" has seemed no longer to apply. Modernism in music may well have begun here, that is, with the inability of composers and listeners—unconsciously, as with a language—to absorb a common grammar and syntax when moving from the music of one composer to that of another, and even from one individual piece to another. Self-conscious "pre-composition" began here: composing from scratch, as it were, Pierre Boulez's brave new worlds of the 1950s and 60s, and the high degree of self-reference or individuality that the American composer Milton Babbitt ascribed to the 12-tone works of Schoenberg.

Is greatness possible among the apples and oranges of today's pluralism? Are unfathomable depths (or structural depths, for that matter) possible without a common language that is absorbed effortlessly by composers and listeners alike? Is language-free music necessarily flat and shallow, a succession of "pretty sounds," as the American theorist Fred Lerdahl proposed in his description of Boulez's Le marteau sans maître (1955)?[1]

By the 1990s, postmodernists had inflicted further uncertainty on a predicament already rife with doubt. Composers were "deconstructed" in their characters, politics, and sexualities. Between the two World Wars, Stravinsky's politics were reactionary (anti-Communist, at the very least), pro-order, pro-tradition, and pro-established religion. He admired Benito Mussolini and fascist Italy for a time. (Later in the United States, he admired Harry Truman.) Are his neoclassical works of the 1930s inflected (or infected) by these socio-political associations? Are they inherently scarred by them? Or is much of this more accurately a question of what the listener may be reading into the music?

And what might the maleness of the Western canon imply, not to mention its whiteness? Is the reach of this music limited by its "lack of diversity" in this regard? The proponents of the New Musicology at the beginning of the 21st century certainly thought so. (Ideas about the autonomy of music, its ability to stand alone and be listened to for its own sake—ideas shared and promoted by Stravinsky for at least a half-century—had by this time receded altogether.)

To follow W. H. Auden, the "modern problem" had to do with

tradition and self-consciousness, with the artist being "no longer supported by a tradition without being aware of it."[2] Composers were no longer able to think creatively—naturally and in good faith, as true believers—in the language of tonal harmony and melody, the materials having become spent through overuse. (The proverbial remedy for overuse, a constant alteration or *individualization* of the materials, could be carried only so far without the system itself breaking down.) The loss of tonality signaled something akin to a loss of innocence, a fall from grace.

One might have expected from all this a stilted and forced character on the part of Stravinsky's neoclassical works, houses divided unto themselves, as it were. But such is not the case. Bach could hardly be more overtly present in 20th-century music than he is in the second movement of Stravinsky's *Capriccio* (1929) and in the "Dumbarton Oaks" *Concerto in E-flat* (1938). Yet this music sounds new and fresh, not broken or contrived. The impression gained is that of a music composed in one fell swoop, in a single sweep of the imagination. It is as if Bach's music, separated from Stravinsky's by two centuries, had been a part of the latter's immediate past. Such is surely a measure of the success of this music, maybe even of its old-fashioned greatness.

1. Years of Apprenticeship

Igor Fyodorovich Stravinsky was born on June 5, 1882, in Oranienbaum (now Lomonosov), a small but fashionable resort town to the west of St. Petersburg on the Gulf of Finland. At the time of his birth, his parents, Fyodor and Anna, had been on vacation. In tsarist times, Oranienbaum had flourished as the summer destination of artists and literary figures. Among the musicians who came and went, Modest Mussorgsky spent his last summer there in 1880. The Stravinsky family returned in 1884 and again in 1885.

The third of four children, all boys, the future composer appears to have been "deeply lonely" and "unhappy" as a child, in need, as he would later recall, of "a sister of my own." When he married his first cousin, Catherine Nosenko, in early 1906, he may have done so at least in part out of a need for sisterly companionship. The two were married in secret, as parallel-cousin marriages were prohibited in imperial Russia. And they remained devoted to each other for the next few decades, notwithstanding the composer's marital infidelities, which were often quite open and bruising in their effect on his immediate family. Two children were born prior to *The Firebird* (1910) and the composer's subsequent relocation to France and French-speaking Switzerland: Fyodor (Theodore), who later became an artist and designer, and Lyudmila (Mika), the first of two daughters.

Family trauma accompanied the composer's early sense of loneliness. The oldest of his four brothers, Roman, died in 1897, while his younger brother, Gury, died of typhus in 1917. Tragedy of this kind was not uncommon at the time, given the state of medical science and, especially, the lack of antibiotics. But it seems to have left its mark all the same. The composer's father died of throat cancer in 1902, while he himself suffered early on from bouts of tuberculosis. Catherine would spend much of her married life in and out of clinics and sanatoriums, battling tuberculosis until finally succumbing to this debilitating disease in March 1939. Stravinsky too suffered a relapse of several months directly following her death.

Scarcely surprising, then, are the grim and unsmiling appearances of the composer and his family in portraits and photographs from this early period of his life. His biographer, Stephen Walsh, would later record something of the gloominess of the general surroundings, the bereavements that could prevail for months on end.[1] At the same time, however, the bleakness of his home life could not have overshadowed altogether the good fortune that was his in many ways. He adored his German governess, Bertha Essert, who would accompany his family to Switzerland in 1910. His parents, cultivated and comfortably well-to-do, lived across from the Mariinsky Theatre in St. Petersburg, on the second floor of an apartment building that still stands today at 66 Kryukov Canal.

For 25 years, the composer's father served as the principal bass singer at the Mariinsky Theatre, site of the Court Opera. He is believed to have performed in some 60 roles, mostly from Russian and Italian lyric operas. Resourceful, Fyodor amassed a library of 7,000 volumes (mostly history and folklore), and adopted what American musicologist Richard Taruskin has called a "scholarly" approach to his operatic roles, designing his own costumes and seeing to his own make-up.[2] Fyodor's technique as a basso was "amazing," as Igor recalled much later, although he was especially prized as a "singing actor."

One can only imagine the concerts and opera productions the young Igor attended, and the many friendships struck up with singers and musicians. He learned at an early age to sight-read at the piano, devouring the vocal scores in his father's library in the process. Improvisation at the piano was another habit picked up in his youth. "I could improvise without end," he confided in his 1908 resume, "and was passionately fond of doing so." From these early years through the entirety of his career, Stravinsky would compose at the piano. "Fingers are not to be despised," he wrote in his 1935 *Autobiography*; "they are great inspirers and, in contact with a musical instrument, often give birth to ideas which might otherwise never have come to life."

Apart from school, the future composer spent much of his youth and early teenage years improvising and studying the piano, the latter from the age of nine with a succession of piano "mistresses." He seems not to have developed as a concert pianist, however, even if, beginning in the mid-1920s in France, this is what he ultimately became—a composer writing and frequently performing his own piano music. While his family likely suspected that Igor would eventually become a musician, they did not actively encourage such an outcome. Instead, they insisted that he attend university in preparation for an appointment in the civil service. Thus, in 1901 he entered the University of St. Petersburg, studying law. Such was the expected path for youngsters of Stravinsky's age and social station, and it was the one his father had taken years earlier in Kiev.

Yet Stravinsky would continue with his studies in music. That same fall he embarked on a series of 14 lessons in tonal harmony with Fyodor Stepanovich Akimenko, a recent student of Rimsky-Korsakov's at the St. Petersburg Conservatory. And the following spring he took up tonal counterpoint with another of Rimsky-Korsakov's students, a study which greatly appealed to him at the time, from species counterpoint to canon, and from invertible counterpoint to fugue. His experiences as a student of practical theory were little different from those of theory students generally over the centuries, whether in Russia or in today's colleges and universities the world over. Genuinely musical results have always been easier to come by in the study of counterpoint than in four-part harmony, which, with its voice-leading rules, is a more complex subject, especially when a figured bass is withheld. Most difficult of the academic exercises has always been the dreaded *chant donnée*: a melody from which students are asked to extract the harmony in four parts and with proper voice-leading intact.

The master and his student

Momentous for Stravinsky during his university years was his first meeting with Nikolai Rimsky-Korsakov. This took place in the summer of 1902 near Heidelberg, Germany, where Rimsky-Korsakov's youngest son, Vladimir, had been studying philosophy. The Stravinsky family was also in Germany at the time, accompanying Fyodor who had been undergoing X-ray treatment for throat cancer. (Sadly, Stravinsky's father failed to improve and died within several months of his treatment.) The meeting with Rimsky-Korsakov was arranged by Vladimir, who had also been studying at St. Petersburg, and where he, his brother Andrei, and Stravinsky had become friends. Rimsky-Korsakov senior must have been pleased by what he heard and saw, for he recommended that Igor continue with his counterpoint lessons and return occasionally for advice. He also invited him to attend his *jours fixes*, musical gatherings that were held every other Wednesday at his apartment in St. Petersburg.

Stravinsky followed through with much of this, becoming a regular at his teacher's *jours fixes*, and then returning from time to time with his compositions. In August of 1904, he returned with his first opus, the Piano Sonata in F-sharp Minor, which was subsequently performed at a Rimsky-Korsakov *jour fixe* on February 9, 1905.

A former Naval officer and "Anglophile," as Stravinsky later remembered him, Rimsky-Korsakov was largely self-taught as a musician. Although something of a cold fish personally, he was patient and generous to the hundreds of students who passed through his theory and composition classes at the Conservatory. Flexible and sensitive to the individual needs of his students, he advised the ill-prepared Stravinsky not to attend the conservatory, but to continue privately on his own. He was methodical as a composition teacher, insisting that all bases be touched, and that musical ideas be thought through logically. (Claude Debussy called him a "voluntary academic, the worse kind," while Rimsky-Korsakov, as if in retaliation, thought of Debussy's music as "decadent"). The year 1905 marked violent anti-government protests and strikes in St. Petersburg, pro-democracy demonstrations in which Rimsky-Korsakov himself took part at the Conservatory. Both the Conservatory and the University were closed for extended periods.

Stravinsky's regularly scheduled lessons with Rimsky-Korsakov began in the fall of 1905, and continued for nearly three years until the latter's death of an asthma attack in June 1908. The lessons were held on Wednesdays at 4:00-6:00 PM; on *jours fixes*, the young composer stayed for dinner. Taruskin reports that Stravinsky had by this time become a virtual member of the Rimsky-Korsakov household, Rimsky-Korsakov himself, something like a substitute father.

Stravinsky's exercises in orchestration were little different from the ones Rimsky-Korsakov had been assigning for years at the Conservatory. We know this from the testimony of his students, in particular Sergei Prokofiev. Included in these exercises were collections of Beethoven's sonatas and Franz Schubert's waltzes; occasionally, he would assign an exercise from his own recent work, which in the case of Stravinsky would have been *The Invisible City of Kitezh* (1907). Stravinsky may have had a hand in the orchestration of this opera's third act.

Composition was another matter. Stravinsky's lessons began with a solidly academic Symphony in E-flat major in four movements and ended with the *Scherzo fantastique* (1908) for large orchestra. The *Scherzo* was followed by a short work, *Fireworks* (1909), which in turn was interrupted for the *Chant funèbre* (1908). Composed in memory of his teacher, the score and parts of the *Chant* were lost for over a century, and not found until 2015 in an archive at the St. Petersburg Conservatory. The melodic motive that opens the *Chant* foreshadows that of *The Firebird* two years later (see example 2.1). The difference lies in the interval that encloses the motive in each case. That interval is a perfect fourth in the earlier *Chant*, a tritone in *The Firebird*. As we shall see in Chapter 2, tritones are key to the melodic and harmonic life of *The Firebird*.

Conceived initially with a program based on Maurice Maeterlinck's book *La Vie des Abeilles*, the *Scherzo fantastique* consists musically of sequences derived from the whole-tone and octatonic scales. In American jazz circles, the octatonic scale is known as the "diminished scale." In this and other ways, the *Scherzo* is conspicuously a product of Rimsky-Korsakov's teachings and of Stravinsky's close familiarity with his teacher's operas and symphonic poems. (Such familiarity would have begun much earlier, of course, when, as a boy, Stravinsky sight-read through his father's vocal scores and attended productions of the Court Opera). The supernatural themes of Rimsky-Korsakov's music, drawn largely from Russian folklore, were invariably accompanied by sequential patterns derived from the two scales mentioned above. The patterns in Stravinsky's *Scherzo* and *Fireworks*, although sometimes more elaborate and inventive than those in Rimsky-Korsakov's operas, are all very much a part of a tradition that stretches back to Mikhail Glinka's *Ruslan and Ludmilla*.

The descending sequence cited from the *Scherzo* in example 1.1a consists of four arpeggiated triads or dominant seventh chords, which are often provided by sustained pitches. These are shown analytically in example 1.1b, while example 1.1c demonstrates the octatonic scale implied by the sequence. The scale is *symmetrical*. It is halved at the tritone, which, in turn, is halved at the minor third. The tritone and minor-third cycles divide the octave *equally*. The passage is thus overtly non-tonal, having little to do with the asymmetry of the diatonic major and minor scales. The triads are not motivated tonally, but are subject to the pulls and attractions of their symmetrical confinement.

In his teachings and classes at the Conservatory, Rimsky-Korsakov always referred to the octatonic scale as the "tone-semitone scale;" his students called it the "Rimsky-Korsakov scale." Apart from the tritone and minor-third intervals, the scale is composed of alternating tones and semitones, steps and half-steps or the reverse—half-steps and steps. In addition, Rimsky-Korsakov called octatonic settings such as the one outlined in example 1.1a, b, and c *harmonic*, given that they featured the triad as the unit of vocabulary; along a *descending* minor-third cycle, triads and dominant sevenths are rooted here on E, C#, Bb, and G. (Minor triads and minor seventh chords transposed along this same cycle also remain confined to the given octatonic scale.)

octatonic scale
stemmed notes = roots of triads

EXAMPLE 1.1a, b, and c: *Scherzo fantastique*, octatonic triads, dom. 7th chords

On the other hand, octatonic settings like the one cited in examples 1.2a, b, and c were called *melodic* by Rimsky-Korsakov, since they featured the minor or Dorian tetrachord as melody; here, (F Eb D C) is transposed down the minor-third cycle to D, B, and G#. Examples 1.3a and b show a form of linkage between the harmonic and melodic: the root, seventh, and fifth of the dominant-seventh chord (first inversion, closed position) become an incomplete or gapped Dorian tetrachord, (E D (C#) B). These linkages form an essential background to the pitch relationships in any number of Russian-period works.

EXAMPLE 1.2a, b, and c: *Scherzo fantastique*, octatonic Dorian tetrachords

EXAMPLE 1.3a and b: *Dorian tetrachord as octatonic-diatonic bridge*

Astonishing as it may be, the octatonic framework outlined in examples 1.1, 1.2, and 1.3 would remain an integral part of Stravinsky's musical thought for nearly the entirety of his life. The triads, dominant sevenths, and minor tetrachords in these examples continued to preoccupy him for the next 12 or so years until the close of the Russian period with works such as *The Wedding*, *The Soldier's Tale*, and the *Symphonies of Wind Instruments*. Works of the neoclassical era confine themselves in large part to the triads and dominant sevenths pictured in examples 1.1a, b, and c. The dominant seventh and its links to the Dorian tetrachord and the modal diatonicism of Russian folk songs (examples 1.3a and b) are more specific to the Russian era.

To be sure, the sound of the octatonic in Stravinsky's music changed over time. Already with *Petrushka* (1911) and certainly with

The Rite of Spring (1913), the octatonic vocabulary shown in examples 1.1, 1.2, and 1.3 began to be superimposed, leading to the creation of new dissonant sonorities. Stravinsky would sometimes arrange the repetition of this vocabulary polyrhythmically, producing cross accents. Or he would place two or more "blocks" of heterogeneous, contrasting material in a kind of abrupt juxtaposition with one another. Such were the techniques with which the octatonic became closely identified in his music, a sound that would prove influential with a great many composers of the past century, including, late in life, Debussy.

For Stravinsky, the source of the octatonic scale was undoubtedly Rimsky-Korsakov, while, for the latter, it was Franz Liszt. And Liszt may have extracted it from symmetrical passages such as the one that opens the Sanctus in Schubert's Mass in E-flat major.

In his autobiography, *My Musical Life*, Rimsky-Korsakov credited a descending sequence in Liszt's first symphonic poem, the *Mountain Symphony* or "Ce qu'on entend sur La Montagne," with having stirred him in the direction of the octatonic. Underlying this sequence was "a scale which subsequently played an important part in many of my compositions." Beginning with *Mlada* (1892), he would become increasingly enamored of the octatonic scale, inventing ever more intricate octatonic models with which to transpose up and down the minor-third cycle.

And therein lay the rub. Too easily and quickly, the scheme became tiresome, mostly because of its symmetry. Confined to a given octatonic scale, transpositions of a motive or chord up or down the relevant minor-third cycle are *exact*. This stands in marked contrast to tonal sequences, which, confined to a given key, allow for considerable variation. The intervals of a diatonic motive or chord transposed sequentially change automatically; minor thirds become major thirds, semi-tones, tones, and so forth. Moreover, there are as a rule only two repetitions of a model in tonal sequences, the model itself followed by two transpositions. (Bach's *Art of the Fugue* contains four-leveled sequences, but they remain exceedingly rare in the music of the 18th and 19th centuries.)

In contrast to tonal sequences, those of Rimsky-Korsakov's plunge methodically through all four nodes of the minor-third cycle; the octatonic model is followed by three exact repetitions. The dry, mechanical quality of many of these sequences is further enhanced in the Rimsky-Korsakov operas mentioned above by a two-plus-two or four-plus-four metrical squareness.

All of which applies to no less an extent to the octatonic sequences in Stravinsky's *Scherzo fantastique*. Here too, exact repetitions of the octatonic model are metrically square. The difference lies in their speed and orchestral virtuosity. The swirling sequences can delight and engage the listener, and the *Scherzo* became somewhat of a crowd-pleaser in the years that followed, serving often as the opener to special Stravinsky programs.

2. To *The Firebird* (1910)

Premiered on the evening of January 24, 1909, the *Scherzo fantastique* was Stravinsky's first public success. It was introduced on a subscription series founded by Alexander Siloti, a conductor and virtuoso pianist; the setting was formal and prestigious. Siloti regularly hired the best ensemble in St Petersburg, which was that of the Mariinsky Theatre, the orchestra with which Stravinsky had been familiar since childhood. The reaction to his music was cordial and supportive. The reviews placed him among the "modernists" or "advanced" musicians of the day, presumably with an ear toward the *Scherzo*'s octatonic chromaticism and orchestral virtuosity. Not all comments were approving, however. In a letter dated January 25, the composer Cesar Cui complained about the "many curious sound effects" in the *Scherzo* and its "pursuit of sheer sonority [and] orchestral effect." This "pursuit" had come at the expense of substance, he argued.[1]

Present that same fateful evening of January 24 was the impresario who, for the next 20 or so years, would be at the forefront of introducing and promoting Stravinsky's music to the world at large. This was Sergei Diaghilev, who had also attended the University of St. Petersburg, and, as a youngster, had been an aspiring composer. Unlike Stravinsky, however, he had met with rejection at the hands of Rimsky-Korsakov. His youthful compositions were pronounced "worse than nonsensical." Stunned, Diaghilev had retreated before resurfacing years later as a collector and promoter of contemporary art, mostly Russian, but also French and Dutch.

With what appears to have been a super abundance of charm, energy, and ambition, Diaghilev launched the art journal *Mir iskusstva* (World of Art) in 1898 and began sponsoring exhibitions, including the exhibit of Russian folk art in Paris in 1900. His tastes were conservative, or at least retrospective, and combined an art-for-art's-sake philosophy with a belief that the future of Russian music lay with an engagement with its folk art, music, and verse. An "enlightened despot" is how Stravinsky later described Diaghilev, "tyrannical" when in pursuit of an artistic vision, yet adept at gauging talent and seeing to its marketable potential. Still later, the composer would liken him to the Irish playwright Oscar Wilde, his imposing frame, wit, and cunning. But Diaghilev could also be unscrupulous and manipulative in his dealings with artists and patrons, qualities that were obviously a good deal less endearing. His close friendship with Stravinsky dimmed during the 1920s, a result of their near-ceaseless quarrels about contracts and financial arrangements. Both would have a hand in the deterioration and final breakdown of the partnership.

Diaghilev turned next to music. Concerts of Russian music and opera were sponsored at the Paris Opera in 1907 and 1908, respectively. Included in 1908 was a lavish production of Mussorgsky's *Boris Godunov*, starring Feodor Chaliapin in the title role. The sets and costumes were designed by Alexander Golovin and Alexander Benois, the latter a writer, painter, and long-time associate (as well as a cousin) of Diaghilev's. Pieced together from fabrics and artifacts that had been collected from across Russia, the designs were sumptuous, if inauthentic from the standpoint of the time and place in question (the production could never have been mounted in Russia). But they appealed to the Parisian appetite for the primitive and exotic.[2]

Both ballet and opera were staged during the following *saison russe* in Paris in 1909. On the strength of the *Scherzo fantastique*, Diaghilev had commissioned Stravinsky to orchestrate a Chopin Nocturne and a Waltz to serve as the opening and closing numbers, respectively, of *Les Sylphides*. A ballet with choreography by Mikhail Fokine, *Les Sylphides* was a huge success not only in 1909, but also later with the Ballets Russes. As in preceding years, a small army of singers, coaches, stagehands, and technicians was imported from Russia. Included among the dancers were Anna Pavlova, Tamara Karsavina, Vaslav Nijinsky, and Fokine himself.

The Firebird

On the prowl again in late summer of 1909, Diaghilev was in pursuit of "a *Russian* ballet," as he called it in a letter to the composer Anatoly Lyadov. "We have Russian opera, symphony, song, dance, and rhythm," he complained, "but as yet no Russian ballet." His newfound interest in the dance was entirely material. Opera had become financially risky, necessitating a change of venue. And it helped that the ballet was then in a state of disrepair, having been neglected by contemporary Russian composers, with the possible exception of Alexander Glazunov. Rimsky-Korsakov thought it "degenerate" as art, primarily because of the role of mime, which he described as "not a full-fledged art form but only an accompaniment to speech."[3] A few years later, Stravinsky would be voicing similar reservations about mime, although more because of the completely subservient position in which musical composition was placed. The ballet lay in wait, as it were, dormant but ready to be revived with fresh talent and enterprise.

However, Lyadov, who had initially expressed interest in Diaghilev's project, withdrew. And, after him, Glazunov did so as well. Indeed, before Lyadov, Nikolai Tcherepnin may also have bowed out after an initial positive response. Consequently, when the commission for *The Firebird* finally did fall to the relatively untried Stravinsky, it did so at least a few times by default. Not until December was a contract signed by the composer, by which time he had been at work for well over a month. Years later he included a recollection of these early days in his *Memories and Commentaries* (1961):

> I had begun to think about *The Firebird* when I returned to St. Petersburg in the Fall, 1909, though I was not yet certain of the commission (which, in fact, did not come until December, more than a month after I had begun to compose; I remember the day Diaghilev telephoned me to say go ahead... Early in November I moved from St.

Petersburg to a *dacha* belonging to the Rimsky-Korsakov family about 70 miles southeast of the city. I went there for a vacation in birch forests and snow-fresh air, but instead began to work on *The Firebird*. Andrei Rimsky-Korsakov was with me at the time, as he often was during the following months; because of this, *The Firebird* is dedicated to him.

In future years, Stravinsky would develop the habit of working closely with his choreographers, preferring to compose with "exact measurements" rather than blank slates. In the case of *Petrushka* and *The Rite of Spring*, he would be co-authoring the scenarios with, respectively, Benois and Nikolai Roerich. *The Firebird* was a very different matter, however. The libretto had been completed well before it had reached Stravinsky. Put together from an assortment of "stock folk-tale ingredients," it had come to the composer ready-made. And this meant that he would be assuming a subordinate role in his collaboration with the choreographer Fokine. Constant meetings between the two were required to coordinate the music being composed with the details of the libretto and with dance steps that had already taken shape. Especially sensitive in this regard were the narrative portions of the ballet, those which required a recitative-type music. These narrative portions would contribute most to the close coordination between music, dance, libretto, and scenery that would catch the attention of the critics in Paris. In the end, *The Firebird* was seen as having been inspired by the ideals of Wagner's *Gesamtkunstwerk*.

It was at this time, too, that Stravinsky began to attend the weekly meetings of Diaghilev's "committee," an outgrowth of the editorial board of *Mir iskusstva* and antecedent in turn of the so-called Directorate of Diaghilev's Ballets Russes. The quotation below is from the recollections of Sergei Grigoriev,[4] for many years, the calm-and-collected *regisseur* (manager) of the Ballets Russes. His recollection is prized as one of the earliest descriptions we have of the young composer. In it, "Nouvel" stands for Valentine Nouvel, an official of the Imperial Court, while "the General" is General Bezobrazov, a patron of the arts:

> From now on Stravinsky began to be present at our committee meetings, and so I met him for the first time. He was rather short, with prominent features and a very serious expression. He took an active part in the discussions especially those on the production of *The Firebird*. His composition of the score went ahead rapidly, and he sometimes played passages over to us. We all listened attentively but, apart from Diaghilev, expressed no opinion. Nouvel did not share Diaghilev's taste for Stravinsky's music, and as for the General, he declared quite frankly that he disliked it and it was unsuitable for dancing. Diaghilev had certainly been right when he warned us that we should find Stravinsky's music new and unusual.

The origins of *The Firebird*'s libretto are complex. Several folk tales from Alexander Afanasyev's *Russian Fairy Tales* appear to have been instrumental, however. Typically, such tales were blunt in their juxtaposition of black and white, evil and goodness, or the magical/supernatural and human sentiment. In *The Firebird*, King Kaschei and his kingdom (the evil component) are pitted against Ivan-Tsarevitch and his rescue of the Princess from captivity. Accompanying the first of these categories, Stravinsky wrote music that was chromatic, often symmetrical in terms of the octatonic scale; accompanying the second category was music that was diatonic and sometimes with borrowed folk tunes harmonized in a quasi-tonal fashion. In this, of course, his overall approach was very much in line with what his predecessors had been.

In addition, the chromatic music of *The Firebird*, formless and improvisational in character, was designed to accompany the mimed portions of the ballet, which in turn were designed to carry the narrative. These portions stood in marked contrast to the diatonic sections, often with folk songs that were dance numbers. The alternation between the mimed and dance numbers in *The*

Firebird mirrors that between recitative and aria in opera. The musical realization of this duality in Rimsky-Korsakov's operas was transferred to *The Firebird* as a ballet.

To the intricacy of these arrangements, however, the composer added yet another complication: leitmotifs. He would acknowledge as much in a lengthy program note to his 1929 pianola version of *The Firebird*. The irony here is that, by 1929, his disdain for Wagner's music and for the system of leitmotifs generally had become widely known. Yet his 1929 program note would mark his most extensive technical analysis of his own music. It would be applied to a Wagnerian method of composition to which he had grown hostile.

The Firebird's intricacies

The opening measures of *The Firebird* afford as good an illustration as any of the work's chromatic/octatonic/"Leit-Musique" music. The Introduction begins with an ostinato in the lower strings; see example 2.1. Spanning a tritone, the ostinato moves back and forth between the pitches Ab and D. Outlined by the brackets in this example are two motives, the first of these consisting of the ostinato's first, second, fourth, and fifth pitches, paired as a major and minor third, and the second of its first four pitches, spanning the tritone. Representing King Kaschei and the Firebird, respectively, these two leitmotifs appear in various guises throughout the score, transposed, inverted, and retrograded (sounded in reverse). The version shown in example 2.2 is from the *Danse infernale* (Infernal Dance), possibly the best known of the suite's dance numbers.

EXAMPLE 2.1: *The Firebird, Introduction; chromatic (octatonic) leitmotifs*

EXAMPLE 2.2: *The Firebird, Danse infernale; the Firebird leitmotif*

Example 2.3 reintroduces the opening measures of the Introduction and continues with a few subsequent passages. At mm. 5-7, another form of the Kaschei motive is introduced in the trombones. Basically, the octave Ab is split at the tritone, each half of this split articulating the Kastchei motive. The resultant configuration can be interpreted triadically as well, in terms of the two oscillating, tritone-related triads, (Bb D F) and (E G# B); see mm. 18-20.

EXAMPLE 2.3: *The Firebird, Introduction*

Crucially, the tritone relation encompassing the two motives imparts none of the urgency or tendency toward resolution one would have expected had its surroundings been tonal. The tritone or symmetrical division of the octave at Ab and D allows each of the complementary intervals, Ab-D and D-Ab, to oppose one another as "equals," to balance each other out, as it were, by virtue of their similitude. And the same holds for the individual pitches Ab and D. Ab, to which a kind of centricity may be assigned, is not a "tonic"; nowhere is its centricity defined by tonally functioning means.

And so, Stravinsky's A-flat minor key signature is beside the point. Indeed, the signature is dropped at m.18 with the return of the configuration at mm.5-7. The Introduction has little to do with the key of A-flat minor, with the scales or the tonally functioning behavior associated with them. This (possibly) first music to be composed in *The Firebird* is *octatonic*. The opening ostinato and its two embedded motives, a design from which much of the ensuing chromatic figuration of *The Firebird* is derived, was conceived within an octatonic framework.

"A novel and highly personal endeavor"

When, in 1919, Stravinsky fashioned an orchestral suite from six dance numbers of *The Firebird*, the music, played the world over, became for a long time the most performed and popular piece of contemporary art music. In his *Memories and Commentaries* (1962), the composer attributed the success of *The Firebird* to its having been "of the styles of its time." The ballet score was "more vigorous than most of the composed folk music of the period," he averred, "but it is also not very original. These are all good conditions for success."

More recently, too, critics and historians have followed suit. The composer's instrumental wizardry has been praised, as well as his "instinctive grasp of the properties of instrumental sound." But the music has been dismissed as conventional and unoriginal, as having been little more than the "culmination" of a dying tradition. "Today," wrote one commentator, "it is easy to hear *The Firebird* as a hodgepotch of kuchkist-type folk-song settings accented a la Borodin," to hear "the sparkling academic ballet style of Glazunov, and a few exoticisms from Rimsky-Korsakov and Scriabin." *The Firebird* is "a veritable monument to the still-revered Rimsky," wrote another, but lacks "any truly great originality."

All of which may be true, of course, but it is partial all the same. The historical record is pursued at the expense of aesthetic reality. For it is only in retrospect, and only in view of the abrupt departures from the tonal tradition that composers like Schoenberg, Webern, Bartok, and Stravinsky were to initiate early in the 20th century, that *The Firebird* is lightly dismissed as a 19th-century cliché. Despite its ties, the music is no more *like* Rimsky-Korsakov than, say, Beethoven's string quartets Opus 18 and 59 are *like* Haydn's. Hence, the historically misleading implications of Stravinsky's explanation of *The Firebird's* success, which he attributed to its having been au courant (up to date), as if composing in "the styles of its day," were a circumstance inherently disadvantageous or not in accord with precedence in Western music generally; as if an explosion like *The Rite of Spring* were "normal"; or as if, too, historical reckoning, any more than analytical-theoretical, could cope with the vicissitudes of public taste and appeal.

Indeed, evidence suggests that, far from having labored as a bundle of conventions, *The Firebird* was in its day deemed a novel and highly personal endeavor. Diaghilev and his committee thought it "new and unusual." And when rehearsals got underway in St. Petersburg, Grigoriev recalled the following:

> Fokine began rehearsals with *The Firebird*, since it was clearly the most difficult of the various works; and Stravinsky was then first introduced to the company. Fokine started on a passage near the middle of the score: the great ensemble called by Stravinsky the *Danse infernale*. From the

> moment they heard the first bars the company were all too dismayed from the absence of melody in the music and its unlikeness to what they were used to dancing to the Mariinsky. Some of them indeed declared that it did not sound like music at all.

And still later, with the orchestra at the Paris Opera, the following:

> Diaghilev invited the well-known Parisian conductor Gabriel Pierne to take charge of the orchestra. Stravinsky attended the orchestra rehearsals and endeavored to explain the music; but energetically though the musicians attacked it, they found it no less bewildering than did the dancers.

Only Taruskin, among today's critics and historians, has examined in considerable detail the chromatic/leitmotif sections of *The Firebird*, praising the inventive ways in which they expand on Rimsky-Korsakov's model. But Taruskin, like the others, found little merit in the mostly diatonic dance numbers of the concert Suite. He, too, concluded that the concert suite "contains little music of interest from a stylistic and historical point of view", and none at all "that gives any inkling of the Stravinsky to come."[5]

But this can hardly be the only way of listening to this early, celebrated music. With the possible exception of the folk-song arrangements in the Khorovod, the music of the Suite still breathes, even after a century of what Stravinsky called "destructive popularity." And it does so as a reflection of the twists and turns he was able to manage even at this early stage of his career.

The Finale of *The Firebird* Suite consists of the constant repetition of a borrowed folk tune. This repetitive construction is remarkable by any standard, even if it is seldom commented upon, so accustomed have we become not only to it, but also to Stravinsky's methods more generally. For there is no mistaking the latter. Masking the repetition are repeated shifts in the song's metrical alignment. At relatively shallow levels of the meter, alignments of the two phrases are displaced. And there are few processes more immediately indicative of Stravinsky's music than these; repeating a motive as a way of displacing it, and displacing it as a way of catching the listener off guard, causing her metrical bearings to be challenged or lost altogether. The impact of much of Stravinsky's music may be felt accordingly.

In example 2.4, the two phrases of the folk song are bracketed and labeled A and B. Below the musical quotation is an outline of the repetition of these phrases for the three sections of the Finale: Lento, Allegro, and Doppio valore. To the left are the rehearsal numbers, to the right, the repetition of the two phrases A and B. The latter phrases are repeated in alternation, as the reader can see, although the repetition is not always strict; A-plus-B (as boxed off) is the standard succession, but in the Allegro, there are sometimes two and even three As to a B and vice-a-versa. And this anticipates, beginning with the opening tableau of *Petrushka*, the block structures of Stravinsky's later works, the technique of slicing up thematic statements into smaller units, and of repeating those units separately and independently of each other.

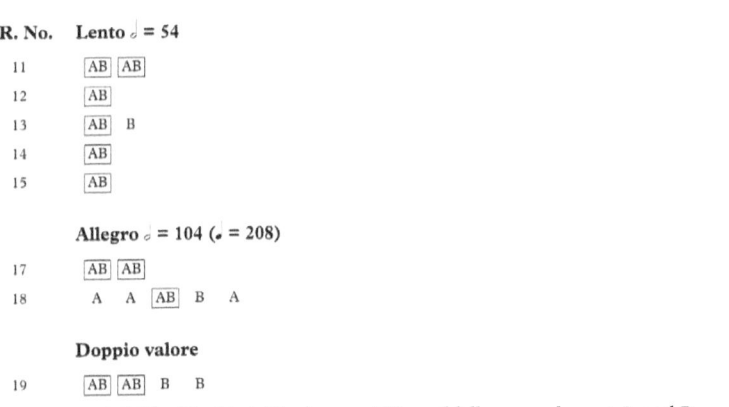

EXAMPLE 2.4: *The Firebird*, Finale: repetition of folk-song phrases A and B

Observe, too, that the repetition of the A-plus-B structure is a feature of the original conception. New in *The Firebird*, however, is the upsweeping quasi-glissando on the final beat of phrase B; see example 2.5b. And still newer is the eventual displacement of this glissando from the third beat of phrase B in the Lento section to the first beat of phrase A in the Allegro; see example 2.5c. This displacement occurs at rehearsal no.17. (Note values are evened out into quarters at this point, while Stravinsky squeezed phrases A and B into two successive 7/4 bars.)**6**

EXAMPLE 2.5 a, b, and c: *The Firebird*, Finale: folk song and its source

Readers of the printed score have tended generally to accept a composer's notation of the meter as an accurate reflection of the listener's experience. At rehearsal no. 17, the assumption is that the displacement will be felt as such; the glissando appears on the downbeat of two successive 7/4 measures. Crucially, however, phrases A and B are no longer metrically parallel. In conflict with the earlier repetition in the Lento section, the folk song's two phrases A and B fall on the second and first beats of the 7/4 bar line, respectively.

And, indeed, listeners could very well respond accordingly. In opposition to the notation, they might be inclined to continue with the alignments of the previous Lento section, sensing the quasi-glissando on an upbeat, that is, on the last beat of phrase B. These listeners will be spared the necessity of switching to the difficult quarter-note beat (with Stravinsky's metronome count of 208 beats per minute); instead, they could continue with the half-note beat, avoiding the notated sevens altogether. To demonstrate how this works, the passage is given in its original form in example 2.6a and rebarred in 2.6b; phrases A and B encompass 3/2 and 4/2 bars, respectively, as the brackets indicate. The glissando beat, accented by the tuba and bass drum, becomes a giant syncopation.

EXAMPLE 2.6 a and b: *The Firebird*, Finale: opening bars of Allegro section, alternative barring

In subsequent sections of the Allegro, the two phrases A or B are repeated separately and independently of each other. The initial phrase A is repeated twice before a return to the A-plus-B pattern. And although, theoretically, listeners could continue to hear the glissando as an upbeat to phrase A, their sense of the half-note beat is likely to be disturbed, with a confrontation with the irregular sevens of the notated score all but inevitable.

The drama of this music, from a rhythmic perspective, unfolds in just this fashion. The metrical displacement of a motive or figure creates a sense of conflict. Either the displacement at rehearsal no.17 is felt as such (as notated, that is), or the repetition of the glissando is felt as being parallel to the original. Either way, however, the alternative to the route taken is likely to surface in the form of a challenge. As the repetition of the two phrases continues irregularly and at a rapid pace at rehearsal no.18, the listener's sense of a meter above the quarter-note beat is likely to be upended altogether. The rhythmic "play" of Stravinsky's music originates often enough with maneuvers of this kind.

3. *Petrushka* (1911)

Ballet; Burlesque in four tableaux by Igor Stravinsky and Alexander Benois. Large orchestra. Dedicated to Alexander Benois. Original choreography by Mikhail Fokine. (First performance, Ballets Russes, Théâtre du Châtelet, Paris, June 13, 1911. Conducted by Pierre Monteux.)

I was called to the stage to bow at the conclusion [of *The Firebird*], and was recalled several times. I was still on stage when the final curtain had come down, and I saw coming toward me Diaghilev and a dark man with a double forehead whom he introduced as Claude Debussy. The great composer spoke kindly about the music. (Igor Stravinsky and Robert Craft, *Memories and Commentaries*)

It was not only Debussy who introduced himself to the young Russian composer in the wake of *The Firebird*'s premiere on June 25, 1910. A host of French writers, artists, and musicians did so as well, possibly at subsequent performances. If we can trust Stravinsky's recollections, the writers included Jean Cocteau and Andre Gide, future collaborators of his, suppliers of the Latin and French texts for, respectively, *Oedipus Rex* (1927) and *Persephone* (1934). These and other more specifically European as well as neoclassical ventures lay not too distantly in the future.

For the moment, however, the sensational success of *The Firebird* had led Diaghilev to schedule supplementary performances. Hurrying back to St. Petersburg to gather his two children, wife, mother, and Gury, Stravinsky returned *en famille* for the final performance on July 7. Rimsky-Korsakov's son Andrei made the trip as well, arriving in time for the same event. His concerns were very different from Stravinsky's, however. They centered on his father's symphonic poem, *Scheherazade*, which had been choreographed by Fokine and paired with *The Firebird* on the same program. Not only had the elder Rimsky-Korsakov's score been cut rather severely

(Diaghilev and Fokine had lobbed off the third movement), but the exaggerated exoticism of the costumes, scenery, and dances were not what had been intended. Andrei wrote to his mother of his distress, and included the following about Stravinsky:

> Igor is floating on air at the success of his ballet, and at the praise which has been and still is being showered on him. He's in raptures over the French, and says that only here do you find real taste and art, etc. He's even talking about emigrating completely. All this makes reasonable people very much shake their heads.[1]

And so it must surely have been. Overnight, at the age of 28, the composer had gained international stardom, and the experience could not but have transformed him. Directly following the premiere, he had been making plans to remain in France for the summer (La Baule, Brittany), and to proceed from there to Lausanne, Switzerland, in September. As it turned out, he and his family would end up in Clarens, on the eastern shore of Lake Geneva, and then, for the winter months, in southern France. The ostensible reason for this European itinerary was the health of his children and, above all, that of his wife, Catherine (or Katya), who had a history of tuberculosis and was expecting her third child. (A boy, Sviataslov or Soulima, was born on September 23 at a clinic in Lausanne.) Medical facilities in Switzerland were superior to those in St. Petersburg, and the climate was thought to be healthier as well.

Quite apart from these personal matters, however, there were professional ones as well. Stravinsky's success had come as a liberation of sorts. No longer so entirely at the mercy of the musical establishment in St. Petersburg (that of the Rimsky-Korsakov clan, more specifically, made up of the composer's family and his many students), Stravinsky was now free to chart his own course. Indeed, in the next few years, his relations with the Rimsky-Korsakovs cooled. Increasingly, he found himself having to defend not only Diaghilev and the Ballets Russes, but also the Parisian public, and, in opposition to opera, the aesthetic value of ballet as an art form. And it was above all the youngest son Vladimir who challenged the composer on these matters, despairing of the ballet as "the lowest form of art." In a letter dated September 1911, Stravinsky replied to Vladimir in the following manner:

> I can only tell you that I, on the contrary, love and am interested in ballet most of all, and this is no empty enthusiasm, but a serious and profound delight in the theatrical spectacle—as living visual art. And I'm simply perplexed that you, who so loved the plastic art and were so keenly interested in painting and sculpture—can pay so little attention to choreography.[2]

Stravinsky's affinity for the dance, intensely felt, would continue through the neoclassical years with *Apollo Musagetes* (1928), *Orpheus* (1947), and *Agon* (1953-57). Each of these would be choreographed by Georgi Melitonovich Balanchivadze, better known almost immediately upon his arrival in the West as George Balanchine. And this list does not include the works choreographed after the fact, as it were—pieces such as the Violin Concerto (1931), which, as a ballet, was renamed *Balustrade* (1941).

But it was the indifference and even hostility of the Rimsky-Korsakov clan toward *Petrushka* that would prove fatal. The clan's impression of this music seems to have been that of a loosely stitched medley of cleverly arranged borrowings, an admixture of Russian folk tunes (of which the clan approved, at least in principle), and Russian street songs and "ditties" (which it believed unworthy of the composer, and certainly of any student of Rimsky-Korsakov's). Quite simply, *Petrushka* was undignified as music and theater, out of step with the serious and formalist path that had been laid down by the composer's teacher. (Upon Stravinsky's request, Andrei Rimsky-Korsakov had forwarded printed copies of the "urban songs" he had been inserting into *Petrushka*. Andrei included a note questioning his right to use such "trash.")

In the years before World War I, the composer would continue to visit St. Petersburg, and to spend his summers in Ustilug, Ukraine, where his family had long maintained a summer home. But he would never truly live in St. Petersburg or Russia again. Rejected for military service because of his tuberculosis, Stravinsky spent the war years exiled in Switzerland. In October of 1917, the Bolshevik coup cut him off from Russia altogether. A French citizen in 1934, he became an American in 1945. But looking still further into the future, on the eve of his return trip and tour of Russia in 1962, he proclaimed his allegiance to his homeland.

> I've spoken Russian all my life, I think in Russian, my way of expressing myself is Russian. Perhaps this is not immediately apparent in my music, but it is latent there, a part of its hidden nature.

Caught up in the moment, no doubt, in the language and sights that had long been left behind, the composer was for a brief period in free fall. As his companion Robert Craft later recalled, however, the toasts and ceremonials turned boozy and surreal in a hurry, and within a few weeks of arriving back in France from Moscow, the tour was quickly forgotten. The homecoming was set aside and bracketed. And for most of the composer's life, it would be in France, Switzerland, and then in California that he would feel reasonably at ease, not only artistically and intellectually, but perhaps even personally as well. Above all else, no doubt, he wished to be left alone. Opportunities for the performance of his music mattered, but it was his ability to compose relatively free of distraction that concerned him most.

Petrushka takes shape

At La Baule, France, Stravinsky was in communication with the Russian painter, writer and archeologist Nikolai Roerich about a scenario for *The Great Sacrifice*. This was *The Rite of Spring* in embryonic form, at least a year before anything concrete had taken shape. While completing *The Firebird* in March, Stravinsky had had "a fleeting vision" of a "maiden" dancing herself to death. This idea was not accompanied by music, but he contacted Roerich anyway, a specialist in the pagan rituals of pre-historic Russia.

Arriving on a visit to Stravinsky and his family in October of 1910, Diaghilev was quite naturally expecting to hear something of the *Sacrifice*. Instead, he was introduced to the beginnings of *Petrushka*, as the following celebrated passage from Stravinsky's *Autobiography* makes clear:

> Before tackling *The Rite of Spring*, which would be a long and difficult task, I wanted to refresh myself by composing an orchestral piece in which the piano would play the most important part–a sort of *Konzertstuck*. In composing this music I had in mind a distinct picture of a puppet, suddenly endowed with life, exasperating the patience of the orchestra with diabolical cascades of arpeggios. The orchestra in turn retaliates with menacing trumpet blasts. The outcome is a terrific noise which reaches a climax and ends in the sorrowful and querulous collapse of the poor puppet.

The *konzertstuck* to which Stravinsky referred above was never completed as such. Diaghilev quickly persuaded him to convert the puppet imagery into a ballet scenario. And this first music to be composed became the second tableau of *Petrushka*, the name for the Russian Punch or Pierrot, an angry and volatile character, as Stravinsky described him above. As the scenario evolved, however, Petrushka would acquire a more sympathetic and tragic-comic image, along the lines of the stock characters in the Italian Commedia dell'arte. Petrushka would also be joined by two other puppets, the Blackamore and the Princess. All three characters would be brought to life by a magic trick at the end of the first tableau, the scene of the Shrovetide fair at Admiralty Square in St. Petersburg (circa 1830). The love triangle would play itself out in the second and third tableaux. The well-known "Russian Dance," also in the first tableau, was composed along with the initial *konzertstuck*.

And the notorious "*Petrushka* chord", the nucleus of the pianos "diabolical cascades of arpeggios" and of the orchestra's "menacing" retaliation, would consist of the two tritone-related triads rooted on F# and C; see examples 3.1a, b, and c. In combination, the "chord" is octatonic, of course, but it is the separation of the two triads, with the one clashing with the other, that most determines the sound of this music. At opposite poles of the circle of fifths, arpeggios of (F# A# C#) and (C E G) pitted the black keys of Stravinsky's piano against the white, his left hand against the right. Such binary oppositions, irreconcilable halves, were designed to complement the quirky antics of the half-real, half-mechanical puppet, a Petrushka grossly maligned, but through his "chord" in the final measure of the fourth tableau, jeering at the cheap sentimentality of the real world of the Moor, the Ballerina, and the Crowd. (The borrowed Joseph Lanner waltz tunes in the third tableau depict insipid or otherwise standardized sentimentality. Stravinsky later expressed a particular fondness for the final exposition of Petrushka's "chord" in the trumpets at rehearsal no. 132, fourth tableau: "I wanted ... to show that his ghost is still insulting the public.")[3]

EXAMPLE 3.1 a, b, and c: *Petrushka*, second tableau, "Petrushka chord"

Stravinsky later claimed that he had conceived of the initial *Petrushka* music "in two keys", presumably, in F# major and C major. This conception of "two keys" would lead to the propagation of terms such as "bitonality" and "polytonality" in the first half of the past century. Darius Milhaud and other composers were led to write piano pieces "in separate keys." But apart from the dubious nature of these notions, especially from a perceptual standpoint (listeners can attend to only one key at a time, even if the clashing of keys may doubtless be felt as an "effect"), there is no simultaneous, tonally functional unfolding of separate keys in *Petrushka*'s second tableau, only an oscillation or superimposition of the tritone-related triads on F# and C.

In other words, it is the superimposition of the two triads (rather than the two keys) that counts. In example 3.1a, the two triadic outlines are superimposed in the clarinets, while a snippet of the composer's "cascades of arpeggios" appears in example 3.1b; the orchestra's "menacing trumpet blasts" are reproduced in example 3.1c, where, in triplets, an outline of a C-major triad is superimposed over (A# C# F#). In examples 3.1a and c, the tritone-related triads no longer *progress* or succeed one another (as they do, harmlessly, in the examples from the *Scherzo fantastique* and *The Firebird* in the previous chapters). They are now imposed *simultaneously*. And the "bite" of the resultant dissonance, from which the most startling implications were to accrue in harmonic, melodic, instrumental, and rhythmic design, opened up a new universe for Stravinsky, a new dimension in octatonic thought, one that he was to render peculiarly his own.

Remarkably, Stravinsky would complete the first and second tableaux of *Petrushka* before meeting up with his librettist, Alexander Benois. The two met for several weeks at Christmas time in St. Petersburg. Corresponding on matters of staging and design over the next few months, he and Stravinsky became co-authors of the scenario. Mercifully for the composer, the chronology was the opposite of what it had been with *The Firebird*; Fokine's choreography would come after the music and the scenario had been completed. Just as with *The Firebird*, Stravinsky attended the preliminary ballet rehearsals, which were held in April and May of 1911. With the orchestra in Paris, however, he would find the musicians as resistant and befuddled as they had been nearly a year earlier. Some laughed openly when confronted with their parts. And the dress rehearsal was no less chaotic. The lighting remained in disarray, the dancers complained about the lack of space on stage, and Fokine and Stravinsky were still quarreling about the tempos. A new argument about the sets had broken out between Benois and Diaghilev.

Yet the first performance of *Petrushka*, held at the Théâtre du Chatelet in Paris on June 13, was a resounding success for Diaghilev and the Ballets Russes. Diaghilev's "genius for brinkmanship" (as Stephen Walsh has described it), his ability to overcome the seemingly insurmountable at the last minute, prevailed once again. The performance succeeded not only musically, but in terms of the design and dance as well. While Nijinsky had been halting and uncertain at rehearsals, his performance in the title role appears by all accounts to have marked an electrifying moment in the history of modern ballet. "But to call [Nijinsky] a great dancer is not enough," Stravinsky added much later. "He was an even greater dramatic actor."[4]

A polyrhythmic way of composing

While seeking to capture in *Petrushka*'s first tableau something of the bustling sound of the Shrovetide fair in St. Petersburg, Stravinsky happened upon a polyrhythmic way of composing that would remain characteristic of his music for years to come. In polyrhythm, two or more rhythms may not be perceived as deriving from one another, or as simple manifestations of the same meter; two or more layers of independently repeating parts may be heard as superimposed in the manner of a *stratification*. There is nothing especially new about this, of course, as polyrhythm may be found not only in Western art music (the hemiola is a familiar example), but also in the music of many other cultures. But Stravinsky's polyrhythmic textures tend to persevere at considerable length, extending through whole sections and even movements of music.

As a means of interpretation, it may be useful, in connection with the opening measures of *Petrushka*, to imagine a spectator approaching the fairgrounds and hearing the repetitive cries of a street vendor in the flutes; see example 3.2. These cries are superimposed over the drone-like hum of the crowd, represented in turn by an ostinato in the horns. Just as they might in street music, a pair of dyads move back and forth like an accordion. The spectator turns away to another block of sound at rehearsal no.1, only to turn back again to the original strand. These blocks of material are phased in and out.

EXAMPLE 3.2: *Petrushka, first tableau, opening; Shrovetide fair*

Continuing with this interpretation, we can imagine the spectator entering the fairgrounds at rehearsal no.3; see example 3.3. He begins to hear the various strands "simultaneously" and more loudly. In example 3.3, the shouts of a carnival barker in the piccolos and oboes are superimposed over a continuation of the drone-like hum in the horns.

EXAMPLE 3.3: *Petrushka, first tableau, stratification; entering the fairgrounds*

However, the two upper strands are now superimposed over a third layer, the repetition of a Russian folk song in the lower strings. Three separate layers are thus active at rehearsal no.3. Polyrhythmically, the accents every other quarter-note beat in the borrowed folk song conflict with the three quarter-note beats of the meter; the two against three is one of the familiar varieties of hemiola common to Western music. The "sevens" of the carnival barker (with a separate 7/8 meter) conflict with the two quarter-note beats of the folk song and the three beats of the meter. There are thus three different "meters" for the three layers at rehearsal no.3, even though, psychologically, the listener can attend to only one of these at any given time, hearing the others as a form of challenge. (Hence the preference always for the term "polyrhythm" rather than "polymeter.")

Crucially, the three separate strands at rehearsal no.3 are not tossed about from one instrument to the next in the form of a dialogue; the motives are not transposed or developed in the manner of the Classical style. Rather, each motive or theme remains confined to its own separate register, keeping to itself in this way.

And the repetition is quite literal. Above all, the harmony is static, lacking any sense of movement from one bar to the next.

Observe, too, the length to which the polyrhythmic texture at rehearsal no.3 perseveres. The motives of the two top layers, the carnival barker and the drone-like hum of the crowd, are derived from the folk song. All three layers, for some 45 measures, anticipate and prepare for the *tutti* and climactic outbursts of the folk song at rehearsal no.5 (see example 3.4).

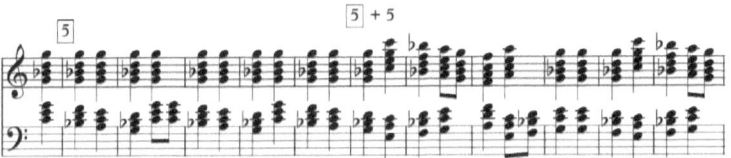

EXAMPLE 3.4: *Petrushka*, I: First tableau; borrowed folk song

The latter is an Easter song, known as the "Song of the Volochobniki". Originally sung by peasant carolers during Easter week, it appears harmonized as such in Rimsky-Korsakov's 100 *National Songs* (1876); see example 3.5. Of interest here are the distinctions in harmonization. While in Rimsky-Korsakov's folk-song collection the melody concludes with a cadence in F major, these tonal allusions are ignored in *Petrushka* (example 3.4). The melody remains centered on the pitch G and the triad (G Bb D), implying the Dorian mode on G. The tune is one of at least 15 borrowings in the four tableaux of *Petrushka*.

EXAMPLE 3.5: *Rimsky-Korsakov's 100 National Songs* (1876), No. 47

It should not be assumed that all musicians and critics in St. Petersburg and Moscow were impervious to the fascination and vitality of *Petrushka*. The young Moscow composer Nikolai Myaskovsky, reviewing the work from a proof score in the journal *Muzika* in January 1912, wrote as follows:

> *Petrushka* is life itself. All the music in it is full of such energy, such freshness and wit, such healthy, incorruptible merriment, such reckless abandon, that all its deliberate banalities and trivialities ... not only fail to repel but, quite the contrary, carry us away all the more.[5]

After the St. Petersburg premiere, Myaskovsky wrote to the 21-year-old Sergei Prokofiev that the music had "turned out still more enchanting than in the score."

4. *The Rite of Spring* (1913)

B allet; scenes (tableaux)of pagan Russia in two parts by Igor Stravinsky and Nikolai Roerich. Large orchestra. Dedicated to Nikolai Roerich. Original choreography by Vaslav Nijinsky. (First Performance, Ballets Russes, Théàatre des Champs-Elysees, Paris, May 29, 1913. Conducted by Pierre Monteux.)

(Rehearsal room, Theatre du Casino, Monte Carlo, April 1912). Stravinsky sat down to play a piano reduction of the entire score [of *The Rite of Spring*]. Before he got very far I was convinced he was raving mad. Heard this way, without the color of the orchestra which is one of its greatest distinctions, the crudity of the rhythm was emphasized, its stark primitiveness underlined. The very walls resounded as Stravinsky pounded away, occasionally stamping his feet and jumping up and down to accentuate the force of the music. My only comment at the end was that such music would surely cause a scandal. (Pierre Monteux, "Early Years").

I decided then and there that the symphonies of Beethoven and Brahms were the only music for me, not the music of this crazy Russian! (Pierre Monteux; quoted in Doris G. Monteux, *It's All in the Music*; see Richard Taruskin, "Resisting *The Rite*," in *Russian Music at Home and Abroad*).

That the first performance of *The Rite of Spring* at the Théâtre des Champs-Elysees in Paris precipitated a riot "must be known to everybody," Stravinsky mused in one of his later books of "conversation" with Robert Craft.[1] Mild protests could be heard early on during the Introduction to *The Rite*. They were followed by a storm of dissent when, at the beginning of the "Augurs of Spring" at rehearsal no.13, the curtain rose on what Stravinsky later described (mockingly) as "a group of knock-kneed and long-braided Lolitas jumping up and down." (Stravinsky disliked the original choreography of *The Rite*, which had been designed by Vaslav Nijinsky, thinking it redundant and too much in step with the music. But he would have to reverse himself when, in 1967, a newly discovered four-hand piano version of *The Rite* with his own choreographic markings revealed dance steps that were indeed often in counterpoint with the music.)

The uproar in the audience continued through the entirety of the first performance, as spectators supportive of the production began shouting and arguing with the protestors. In a rage, Stravinsky left the hall and arrived backstage to find Diaghilev flicking the house lights in an attempt to restore calm. Unable to follow much of the music, the dancers had turned for direction to Nijinsky, who "stood on a chair shouting numbers to the dancers, like a coxswain."

But this celebrated tale of a music first scorned but soon thereafter reclaimed in triumph has had to be amended. For it appears that, to a far greater extent than Stravinsky's score, it was the unorthodox character of Nijinsky's choreography that caused the audience to erupt in protest. (Evidence suggests that the promotional material circulated by Diaghilev and the theater management in the weeks leading up to the premiere may also have had a hand in souring the audience.) Much of the music seems to have been drowned out by the furor, in any case. Seeing everything, the audience may ultimately have heard very little. This is borne out by the critical reviews that followed on the morning after. Attention therein is focused almost entirely on the ballet. Some reviews acknowledge the composer, but make no mention of the music.

Moreover, when *The Rite* was shifted to the concert hall a year or so later (with the ballet eliminated altogether, in other words, but with Pierre Monteux conducting, this time at the Casino de Paris), the outcome was just the opposite of what it had been initially. The audience responded enthusiastically—indeed, to such an extent that the composer was cheered and led triumphantly from the concert hall on the shoulders of several attendees; a celebration ensued outside the hall, as policemen were called in to restore order. ("Our little Igor", Diaghilev quipped, "now needs police escorts out of his concerts, like a prize-fighter.")

The 1914 concert-hall success of *The Rite* was repeated in the capitals of Europe and North America, and even in Soviet Russia in Leningrad and Moscow in 1926. One of the few exceptions to this success was a still earlier performance in Moscow in February of 1914, led by Sergei Koussevitzky. The reading appears to have faltered owing to the lack of rehearsal time. In future years there would be technical, performing difficulties, to be sure, starting with *The Rite's* very first note, the high C in the bassoon solo that opens the Introduction. During the 1920s and 30s, especially, many leading orchestras shied away from this music. However, when portions of *The Rite* were adopted by Walt Disney in his animated film, *Fantasia* (1940), the score's popularity soared. *The Rite* became that rare bird in the annals of the avant-garde of 20th-century music—a spectacular success with both the general public and a multitude of professionals, including composers, academics, and critics.

The creation of *The Rite of Spring*

The actual making of *The Rite* began in July 1911, when Stravinsky traveled to Russia to meet with his co-librettist, Nikolai Roerich, the painter and specialist in Russian pre-history. It was assumed from the start that the scenario of *The Rite* would be more or less plotless, consisting of a series of loosely connected enactments of imagined pre-historic rites. Yet the content of the ritual enactments as dance movements, along with their titles and successions, had yet to be decided. The larger frame of *The Rite* would be divided into two parts representing day and night, "The Adoration of the Earth," followed by "The Sacrifice.". In the form of the "Sacrificial Dance," the original vision of a young maiden "dancing herself to death" would come climatically at the end of Part II.

The first sketches of *The Rite* were those of the "Augurs of Spring," ideas that would find their way into the score at rehearsal no.13. These early jottings occupy the first pages of illustration in Stravinsky's sketchbook at the time, a facsimile of which was published in 1969. But the composition of *The Rite* would not truly get underway until October, when Stravinsky and his family moved from Ustilug back to Clarens, Switzerland. There, in rented housing—with just a tiny closet-like space into which a muted upright piano and a table had been squeezed—*The Rite* was composed very nearly from start to finish. Except for the "Ritual of Abduction," the dance movements were written in the order in which they now appear. The Introduction to Part I, with its famous bassoon solo at the outset, was composed after the dance movements of this part had been completed. Contour-wise, the bassoon melody is a fairly accurate transcription of a Lithuanian folk song, pegged at the time from an anthology of such songs, *Litauische Volks-Weisen*. Scattered throughout Part I are at least four additional borrowings from this source.

In mid-March of 1912, Stravinsky traveled to Monte Carlo to meet with Diaghilev and Nijinsky, who would be assuming the role of choreographer, and to play through Part I and much of Part II of *The Rite*. It was then that he learned of Diaghilev's decision to postpone *The Rite*'s production until 1913. Resources of the Ballets Russes had been stretched, and the fear—justified, as it turned out—was that *The Rite* would prove both expensive and time-consuming. At *The Rite*'s first performance, the standard orchestra of the Ballets Russes had to be augmented by 19 members. Early on, Diaghilev had promised the composer a huge orchestra, and Stravinsky had taken full advantage of this offer.

The composer would later claim that the rehearsals of *The Rite* had transpired without intimation of the riot it precipitated. In fact, he was absent from the initial orchestral rehearsals that were held in late March with the conductor, Pierre Monteux, who sent word on March 30 of several troublesome spots involving matters of balance with the brass instruments. The composer responded promptly with a handful of revisions.

Yet Stravinsky's absence from Monteux's early rehearsals remains something of a mystery. No doubt, he had been preoccupied with last-minute changes, and with the scoring of Mussorgsky's opera, *Khovanshchina*. Earlier in November and December of 1912, however, he had interrupted work on several occasions to assist Nijinsky at dance rehearsals. And his travels with the Ballets Russes could not but have awakened within him an awareness of the many novel technical and interpretative problems attending the performance of his music.

Robert Craft has speculated that Stravinsky might at the time have become apprehensive about the "actuality" of *The Rite*; that, in these final months, he had preferred to work through Monteux, a trusted intermediary. *The Rite* was, after all, "unlike anything he (or anyone else) had ever wrought."[2] Yet the decision not to attend the early rehearsals may have been a practical one. They would almost certainly have stimulated the urge to revise further, and the composer, having labored for nearly a year and a half on the detail of this music, may well have sensed that any tampering on the eve of the premiere (beyond that recommended by Monteux) would prove counterproductive. He may quite possibly have deemed it prudent to wash his hands of the venture temporarily.

In due course, however, Stravinsky would again be answering the call to revise. In preparation for a performance of *The Rite* in Amsterdam in February 1926 (with Stravinsky himself conducting *The Rite* for the first time), he divided the lengthy 8/4 and 7/4 measures of the "Evocation of the Ancestors" into smaller units. He had wanted to facilitate the performance of this music, but the shorter divisions changed the melodic structure as well, revealing a motivic life that had been obscured by the earlier notation. These and other modifications were included in a revised edition of *The Rite* published in 1929 by Russische Musikverlag (later, Edition Russe de Musique), Stravinsky's principal publisher during the 1920s. The firm had been founded by Koussevitzky and his wife, Natalie, in 1909.

Before long, this revised version of *The Rite* would be followed by its own path of corrections and emendations. In 1943, in anticipation of a performance of *The Rite* by the Boston Symphony Orchestra (unrealized), Stravinsky doubled the overriding 16th note of the "Sacrificial Dance" to an easier-to-read eighth note. But the results, which included changes in the instrumentation, were published separately in 1945, and were not made a part of the 1948 edition of *The Rite* published by Boosey and Hawkes. Conductors have tended to ignore this new version of the "Sacrificial Dance," although Stravinsky himself, after its publication in 1945, always included it in his performances of *The Rite*.

For much of his career, the composer was dogged by a publication hitch; neither the United States nor Russia signed the Berne International Copyright Convention, a delinquency that left his music unprotected in these locales. In the United States, popular works such *Petroushka* and *The Firebird* Suite were performed virtuously free of charge for decades. The lost royalties, recouped, "would have made me a millionaire," Stravinsky quipped during the 1960s, carefully adding, however, that for the good of his "soul," he "aspired to no such thing." Nevertheless, his inability to profit from these fruits of his labor would contribute mightily to the embittered edginess of his relations with agents, producers, and publishers. His quarrels with these latter, as revealed in his published correspondence, are an unattractive slice of his biography.

It should come as scant surprise that harmony in *The Rite* should consist of triads and dominant-seventh chords, melody in turn of the Dorian or minor tetrachord. Further: that this vocabulary of triads and tetrachords should be superimposed in the manner of the "*Petrushka* chord"; that the dissonance of *The Rite* should arise accordingly; that the vocabulary and its superimposition should often be octatonic in conception, sometimes diatonic in terms of the Dorian mode; that the swarm of ostinatos in *The Rite* should often be conceived as separate layers in stratifications or polyrhythmic textures; and that many of the dance movements of *The Rite* should indeed be composed of such stratifications.

For all the touted complexity of *The Rite*, in other words, its materials and methods are consistent and straightforward, very much in keeping with what had preceded it in *The Firebird* and *Petrushka*. The difference is that, in *The Rite*, these materials and practices are *maximized* (a term I borrow from Richard Taruskin), magnified, or pushed to a kind of limit. *The Rite* is louder and heavier than most of Stravinsky's other works, while its prolonged dissonances are harsher. Its polyrhythmic textures are thicker and lengthier as well. Thus, the stratification beginning at Rehearsal no.37 in the "Ritual of Abduction" ends up with as many as 10 separate layers of melodic fragments repeating according to varying spans or cycles. *The Rite* is also the most heavily octatonic of Stravinsky's works, except possibly the first movement of the *Symphony of Psalms* (1930), *Babel* (1944), and lengthy sections in the Symphony in Three Movements (1945).

Typical of the sound of this music is the sustained, compound chord at the beginning of the "Ritual of Abduction"; see example 4.1. In the trumpets and horns, respectively, a dominant-seventh chord rooted on Eb is superimposed over a C-major triad. Together with the F# in the timpani, the entire configuration yields the octatonic scale shown below in example 4.1. Then, superimposed over this octatonic component is a reiterating diatonic/modal fragment in the flutes. This, too, is a folk song drawn from the Lithuanian collection cited just above.

EXAMPLE 4.1: *The Rite of Spring*, "Ritual of Abduction," opening; superimposed triads

Combining octatonic harmony, superimposition, and dissonance

Questions may well have surfaced here and in earlier chapters about the viability of the musical quotation in this volume and the analytical commentary accompanying it. To what extent are the sorts of musical relationships surveyed above in example 4.1 *heard* by everyday listeners? Objectively speaking, of course, we as listeners *hear* everything. But what about the specifics of these relationships? While we pursue these matters of perception with an ear and eye toward *The Rite* and Stravinsky's works generally, we should note that they are of a general nature and could just as easily have been pursued on behalf of the materials of another composer.

Some experts, including the music theorist Kofi Agawu, have voiced considerable skepticism about the possibility of the symmetrical defined, octatonic triads and their superimposition in *The Rite* and other Stravinsky works entering the everyday listening experience (unprodded by theory or analysis, in other words). But hearing is a complex matter, as Agawu himself admits. The inability of the layman (or professional, for that matter) to identify explicitly or in music-theoretical terms the Stravinsky phenomena cited above is no reason to believe that these phenomena do not impose themselves on the listener's imagination in one way or another. Much theory and analysis may well be a specification of what is heard by ordinary listeners, subconsciously or without acknowledgment. And analysis is a two-way street. According to the philosopher Kendall Walton, *noticing* a superimposition of triads, perceiving the relationship while acknowledging one's perceiving of it, can have a profound effect on the listener's appreciation or "aesthetic gratification."

Indeed, the assumption here is that the superimposition or *clashing* of triads—so fundamental to the dissonant sound of *The Rite* and many other of Stravinsky's Russian-period works—forms an integral part of our *experience* of this music. At Rehearsal no.37 in example 4.1, the two superimposed entities, (Eb Db Bb G) in the trumpets over a C-major triad in the horns, are kept apart in their registers and instrumental assignments. And they are so as separate layers in the opening pages of the preceding "Augurs of Spring." In some fashion, then, we as listeners *hear* superimposition. The triads, dominant sevenths, and minor tetrachords brought together in the form of a clash in *The Rite* are entities that, earlier in the music of Stravinsky's immediate past, succeeded one another expressively in the form of a progression. Something of a shock may therefore accompany our experience of these techniques of superimposition, the sense, quite possibly along with it, of an old and familiar vocabulary turned on itself. We can imagine *The Rite* as *aggressive* music in these respects.

At the same time, the clashing of triads (see example 4.1) undermines harmonic implication, the sense of movement that each triad may embody individually when placed within a tonal framework. Stravinsky's superimpositions are static "coagulations," as Pierre Boulez described them, and they negate a sense of motion or development. To follow the critic-philosopher Theodor Adorno here as well, Stravinsky wrote "music against music" in the sense that he sought to defy what is musically inherent, namely, "succession." "As a temporal art," Adorno explained,

> Music is bound to the fact of succession and is hence as irreversible as time itself. By starting it commits itself by carrying on, to becoming something new, to developing. What we may conceive of as musically transcendent, namely the fact that at any given moment it has become something and something other than it was, that it points beyond itself—all that is no mere physical imperative dictated by some external authority. It lies in the nature of music and will not be denied.[3]

The combination of an octatonic vocabulary, superimposition, and dissonance in *The Rite* was unknown to audiences in 1913, and indeed is without parallel in the music of Stravinsky's contemporaries. No equivalent to the sound of this combination can be found in Schoenberg's works of "extended tonality," for example, or in the freely dissonant music of the Second Viennese School. The traditions enveloping the atonal and serial repertories of this school are for the most part foreign to *The Rite*. Thus, the spread of a dissonant major seventh at the rehearsal no.13 in the "Augurs of Spring" lies *between* the individual triads or reiterating fragments (see the superimposed triads (Eb Db Bb G) and (C E G) in example 4.1). The origin of this dissonance rests not with the chromatically altered chords in the music of Liszt or Wagner, but rather with the *superimposing* of unadulterated triads, dominant sevenths, and Dorian tetrachords—the latter a mostly octatonic vocabulary inherited directly from Rimsky-Korsakov.

Moreover, what Schoenberg called *developing variation*—the processes of motivic development this composer associated with Brahms and the music of the Classical style more generally—has even less relevance in this context. In developing variation, motivic features are altered as part of an overreaching train of thought. Yet the very melodic, harmonic, and rhythmic characteristics heavily engaged by the developmental processes traced by Schoenberg are precisely those that, in The Rite of Spring, are often retained literally from one motivic repeat to the next. And there is a reason for the retention of these characteristics when, in The Rite and indeed in much of Stravinsky's music, themes, motives, and chords are repeated. The lack of variation in harmony and melody allows the rhythmic scheme (above all, the shifts in the metrical alignment of these entities) to stand in relief. The absence of change in one realm acts as a backdrop for the changes that occur in another.

"Crimes against grace"

On the night of the premiere, the circle of "knock-kneed and long-braided Lolitas" jumping "up and down" were doing so in coordination with the pounding of a single chord at rehearsal no. 13, the outset of the "Augurs of Spring." The scene was nearly the first to be witnessed by the audience, the curtain having risen only moments before. Critics on the following day were no less displeased by Nijinsky's choreography than Stravinsky had been, thinking the dances heavy and even ugly, "crimes against grace." Least sympathetic were the dancers, who denounced Nijinsky's designs as "unnatural" and "constraining." Nijinsky worked with compact groups of dancers rather than individuals, taking advantage of the repetitive and jerky gestures in the score itself. Such would be the case with his sister as well, Bronislava Nijinska, in her designs for The Wedding a decade later in 1923.

The inspiration for the jumping at rehearsal no.13 came in the form of a chord-repetition, as we have noted, arguably the most famous (as well as notorious) eight-bar phrase in all of 20th-century music; see example 4.2. The length of the phrase (eight measures) is conventional, of course, but the accompanying pattern of accents had never before been heard (or *felt*, more specifically) in Western art music.

A single dissonant chord (another triadic superimposition, as it happens) is repeated 32 times in rapid succession. The regularity of this hammer-like action serves as a backdrop for a highly irregular pattern of accents. In example 4.2, these accents are shown above the beams, while the spans between them are marked off by brackets. The numbers above the brackets mark off the number of eighth-note beats encompassed by each span. Readers unfamiliar with musical notation may nonetheless follow the argument by following the series of numbers.

EXAMPLE 4.2: *The Rite of Spring*, "Augurs of Spring," opening bars

The novelty of this invention can still startle. While the bracket totaling three eighth-note beats appears twice, none of the other spans are repeated. The theorist Matthew McDonald has traced the irregular spans bracketed in example 4.2 to the intervals of a triadic superimposition at rehearsal no.14; to follow his logic, Stravinsky converted the intervals of this configuration into semitones and from semitones to eighth-note beats.[4] To follow Taruskin, on the other hand, the irregular accents were designed to represent the "randomness of nature."

In point of fact, the extreme irregularity of these accents goes beyond randomness. According to David Huron, a psychologist who has given much thought to the issue of expectation in music, the accentual pattern at Rehearsal no.13 in *The Rite* is "not just improbable, but less predictable than a random pattern of accents."[5] (Yes, to some degree, probability or predictability is measurable.) And this points to compositional intent, to the attempt on Stravinsky's part to run counter to the 2/4 meter.

Perversely, Stravinsky's accentual pattern at the outset of "Augurs of Spring" was conceived *in opposition* to the 2/4 meter. Rather than merely non-metrical, the pattern is *anti-metrical*. Or, to use Huron's term, the irregular accents and spans in Example 4.3 are "contrametric" in their effect. They were designed to counter and ultimately to disrupt the listener's sense of the 2/4 meter.

At the same time, however, Huron overlooks the five-fold repetition of the ostinato pattern just prior to rehearsal no.13 (again, see example 4.2). Crucially, listeners may carry something of the parallelism of this repetition into the opening bars of this passage, hearing the first two accents as written, that is, as syncopations off the quarter-note beat. Disruption is apt to set in when these accents are shifted to the beat, however. A few bars later, the accents fall on the downbeat. Consequently, here again, it is the metrical displacement of a motive, chord, or accent that lies at the heart of the disturbance.

5. The Swiss Years (I); *The Wedding* (Les Noces) (1917-23)

Ballet; Russian choreographic scenes (tableaux) with song and music; four-part chorus (SATB) with four soloists; orchestra of percussion with four pianos. Original choreography by Bronislava Nijinska. Dedicated to Sergei Diaghilev. First performance, Ballets Russes, Théâtre de la Gaîté Lyrique, Paris, 13 June 1923. Conducted by Ernest Ansermet.

The Wedding is a suite of typical wedding episodes told through quotations of typical talk. The latter is always ritualistic. As a collection of clichés and quotations of typical wedding sayings it might be compared to one of those scenes in *Ulysses* in which the reader seems to be overhearing scraps of conversation without the connecting thread of discourse.

At the first performance in Paris [13 June 1923], the four pianos filled the corners of the stage, thus being separated from the percussion ensemble and the chorus and solo singers in the pit. Diaghilev argued for this arrangement on aesthetic grounds—the black, elephantine shapes were an attractive addition to the décor—but my original idea was that the whole company of musicians and dancers should be together on stage as equal participants.

When I first played *The Wedding* to Diaghilev, he wept and said it was the most beautiful and most purely Russian creation of our Ballet. I think he did love *The Wedding* more than any other work of mine. That it is why it is dedicated to him. [Igor Stravinsky and Robert Craft, *Expositions and Developments*.]

Enthusiasts of Stravinsky's music harbor a special fondness for *The*

Wedding. "The Wedding ranks high in the by no means crowded company of indisputable contemporary masterpieces," wrote Robert Craft in The New York Review of Books (1972). Even Constant Lambert, among the crankiest of the composer's early critics, found something uniquely compelling: "The Wedding is one of the masterpieces of this Russian period and possibly the only really important work that Stravinsky has given us".[1]

And it may be that this miracle of miracles, begun in 1914 but not completed with its fourth and final instrumentation in place until 1923, still offers today's listeners something truly startling. So it would seem, at any rate, regardless whether The Wedding is perceived as a piece of pure music (its battery of percussion with four "elephantine" pianos; see above), or as a musical-dramatic spectacle (its "cantata-ballet" scheme). Certainly, the prolonged indecision in instrumentation was uncharacteristic of Stravinsky, who generally orchestrated while he composed, whatever the preliminary sketch routine. The hesitation can suggest novelty even for the composer of The Rite of Spring, a musical-dramatic inspiration for which there was no ready settlement along lines even remotely traditional. And the difficulties can seem all the more extraordinary given the self-imposed interruptions for Renard (1916) and The Soldier's Tale (1918), pieces of considerable duration and diversity. For Stravinsky was loath to postpone. Once assured of a "find," a melodic or rhythmic idea of some sort, his instinct was to persevere from start to finish, without interruptions. As he later explained, the future seemed never to furnish the certainty of the present. Ideas were best encouraged when new and fresh.

The birth of The Wedding—initially another big piece for Diaghilev and the Ballets Russes—was not unlike that of The Rite of Spring. The idea for a choral work on the subject of a peasant wedding had occurred to the composer early in 1912; the title, Svadebka or "Little Wedding," had come along with it. But The Rite would be followed first by the second and third acts of Stravinsky's early opera, The Nightingale (Act I had been completed in 1909). And the second and third acts of The Nightingale would be followed by the Three

Pieces for String Quartet (1914), a set of short and highly eccentric miniatures.

The first of the *Three Pieces* affords the listener as scintillating an exercise in the mechanics of *stratification* as any in Stravinsky's music. A folk-derived melody in the first violin spans 23 quarter-note beats and is repeated four times; see the brackets in example 5.1. The repetition of this melody is superimposed over ostinatos in the viola and cello spanning seven quarter-note beats. By contrast, the spans between repeats of the Dorian tetrachord in the second violin are irregular; they intrude abruptly and double forte on the context as a whole. The reader may follow these conflicting spans by tracing the overlapping brackets in example 5.1. The numbers represent the number of quarter-note beats encompassed by the bracketed spans. The shifting bar lines are not a meter, strictly speaking, but only the subdivisions of the span encompassing the ostinatos in the viola and cello parts.

EXAMPLE 5.1: *Three Pieces for String Quartet, No. 1; stratification*

And as if the separation between these four string parts were somehow insufficiently underscored, Stravinsky assigns each a different mode of attack: *avec toute la longueur de l'archet* (with the entire length of the bow) for the first violin, *ff* and *sur le sol du talon* (at the heel of the bow) for the second violin, and pizzicato for the cello. The end result is a musical regimentation exceedingly stiff, rigid, and mechanical in conception.

But such, as we have seen in previous chapters, is the nature of the beast. From one bracket to the next in example 5.1, there are few, if any, changes or variations in melody, overall harmony, dynamics, or instrumentation. All is locked in from the start, as it were. What counts in Stravinsky's stratified, polyrhythmic settings are the changing alignments between the repeating fragments and patterns, as each fragment relates to the others and to the meter. Moreover, if these alignments are to make themselves felt, then their articulation must be clean and the meter must be strictly maintained. As far as pitch is concerned, the setting is not overtly octatonic, even if the scale may be heard between the A-G concluding figure of the first violin, F#-E-D#-C# in the second violin, and the Eb-Db-C motive in the cello: in descending order, A-G-F#-E-Eb-Db-C. Against the polyrhythmic separation between the four parts, the octatonic scale binds them harmonically.

That the general public, modestly informed of the string quartet literature of the 18th and 19th centuries, should have found these *Three Pieces* outlandish in the extreme, goes pretty much without saying. In his book, *The New Music* (1924), the critic George Dyson complained: "If this type of passage has any proper place in the art of the string quartet, then the end is near."

Later in the past century, however, the stratification in the first of the *Three Pieces* and the many others like it in *The Rite* and in Stravinsky's subsequent works would exert an influence on the American minimalist composers, Steve Reich and Philip Glass. In the opening pages of John Adams's *El Dorado* Symphony (1991), the stratified fragments in the first of the *Three Pieces* are explicit and hard to miss. On the other side of the spectrum, the attempt to individualize and isolate the four string parts from one another is stretched still further in the five string quartets of Elliott Carter. In the latter, the four parts are assigned different tempos, and lack, as a result, metrical points of intersection.

The Wedding: "Ethnologically true and thoroughly modernist"

To condense Robert Craft's outline of the intricate circumstances surrounding the making of *The Wedding*: work on the libretto commenced in May or June of 1914.[2] In need of additional source texts, Stravinsky traveled to Russia (Ustilug and Kiev) in July of 1914, where he acquired P.V. Kireyevsky's volume of Russian wedding songs (1911), which would serve as the principal source for the libretto. Then, back in Clarens, Switzerland, the song cycle *Pribaoutki* (1914) came first. By the end of November, however, "Stravinsky had drafted some, possibly most, of the music of the first tableau."

Much of 1915 passed with *The Wedding* and the chamber opera *Renard* incubating in what Craft has described as Stravinsky's "amazingly compartmented mind." In January of 1916, the composer accepted a commission for *Renard*, and *The Wedding* was set aside for seven months. Not until October of 1917 was the sketch-score of *The Wedding* complete.

Nearly five years of experiments followed, with varied instrumental ensembles, including percussion groups, imagined peasant bands, pianolas, cimbaloms, and even a harmonium. The problem was only superficially an instrumental one, for it involved the composer's attempt to reconcile the ethnologically true with a thoroughly modernist compositional style. In the final score of April 1923, the four pianos were "impersonal" and "homogenous," as Stravinsky described them, while the percussion section represented an attempt to replicate the sound of a peasant band. And so from the time of *The Wedding*'s conception to its completion nearly a decade passed. Indeed, of all of Stravinsky's works, Craft estimated that "*The Wedding* underwent the most extensive metamorphosis." This oeuvre may not only have preoccupied the composer for the longest time, but may also, in aggregate, have taken him the longest time to compose.

But if this prolonged insolvency was indicative of novelty, of musical ideas that were incapable of succumbing to any ready settlement, it reflected an important development in Stravinsky's musical thought: from 1914 onward, a shift occurred from the immense orchestral resources that had been harnessed on behalf of the *Scherzo Fantastique*, *The Firebird*, *Petrushka*, *The Rite of Spring*, and *The Nightingale* (all reflecting, as Stravinsky noted, "the Russian orchestral school in which I had been fostered"),[3] to the solo-instrumental style of the more modest chamber groups assembled for the *Three Pieces for String Quartet*, *Pribaoutki*, *Renard*, and *The Soldier's Tale*.

Folk traditions behind *The Wedding*

The scenario of *The Wedding* underwent something of a metamorphosis of its own. Early sketches contain musical characterizations and dramatic actions conceived along quasi-operatic lines. They appear to have been composed in coordination with a three-act scenario, one that incorporated a great many of the 17 or so ritual episodes of the folk-wedding play, the *svadebnaya igra*. (By 1913, the imagined time of *The Wedding*, the ritual episodes that lay behind it had evolved into a kind of play, for whose production wedding parties regularly hired a cast of professional actors and singers.)

The nature of these ritual episodes could vary considerably from one district in Russia to another. Central to the play and to Stravinsky's adaptation of it was the *devichnik*, a kind of bridal shower, which usually took place on the day prior to the wedding ceremony. Central to the *devichnik*, in turn, were forms of lamentation—formulas of lament and weeping by the bride and her entourage. In the original conception, a married woman would lead the maidens in the singing of a lament, while covering the bride's head with a veil. The centerpiece of the *devichnik* was the undoing and combing out of the bride's braid (*kosa*), which was then redone in two plaits, wound around her head, and covered with a kerchief that would remain part of her dress for the remainder of her married life.

Soon enough, however, the early three-act scenario was followed by a scaled-down version in which the idea of a narrative account was gradually replaced by that of a synthesis or crystallization. In particular, the *devichnik*, assigned to Act II in the initial scenario, was moved to the start. Stravinsky's play would begin with the ceremony in full swing, as it were, with a lament on the subject of the bride and her farewell to maidenhood. An outline runs as follows:

> PART I
> **First tableau**: At the Bride's
> The tableau opens with the soprano solo singing the Bride's lament.
> **Second tableau**: At the Groom's
> The Groom's curls (*kindri*) are combed, with the groomsmen in attendance.
> **Third tableau**: Seeing off the Bride
> As the Bride departs, the mothers of both Bride and Groom lament the loss of their children to marriage.
> PART II
> **Fourth tableau**: The Wedding Feast
> In the midst of the celebration (*krasniy stol*), the marriage bed is prepared and the newlyweds depart from the feast.

The final version of the scenario was thus an encapsulation. It sought to evoke—in a moment's time, impressionistically—something of the sense and sensibility of the ancient rituals, much as a snapshot might capture the character as well the circumstances of a scene recalled from memory. The libretto was formed in the same fashion. Pieced together from "quotations of typical wedding sayings," the idea here, too, had been to cut and paste, to select in bits and pieces from the Kireyevsky volume of 1,043 wedding songs. Often enough, the verses assembled in this way resembled scraps of conversation, the sorts of lines a shadow narrator of this tale might be imagined as having overheard incidentally when passing from one wedding ceremony to the next. As a form of embodiment, too, a synthesis of what had been passed down through the ages, these same verses represented the "wedding sayings" not of single, individual characters, but of a multitude of brides, grooms, bridesmaids, parents, and guests. To follow what must surely have been Stravinsky's logic at the time, this was a general characterization that in musical terms could best be addressed flexibly rather than in fixed, one-on-one alignments with the vocal soloists. "Individual roles do not exist in *The Wedding*, the composer remarked in *Expositions and Developments*, "only solo voices that impersonate now one type of character and now another." Thus, the soprano impersonates a bride's voice in the first tablelau, that of a goose later in the fourth.

A technically intricate score

The separations between character and character type, and between personal feelings and the feelings to which the rituals themselves make reference, are integral to Stravinsky's adaptation of the *svadebnaya igra*. In the opening of the first tableau (see example 5.2), the bride weeps not out of heartfelt inclination, but out of personal and social obligation. Weighted down by traditions, family, and society, she weeps "because, ritualistically, she *must* weep," as Stravinsky expressed it.

EXAMPLE 5.2: *The Wedding*, first tableau, opening

And such, too, are the details with which Stravinsky's score is often intimately in tune. In the soprano's three-note melodic motive that opens the first tableau, (E D B), the grace-note F#, sliding glissando-like into the motive's lower D, allows for the suggestion for a gasp or sob.

Indeed, from a more strictly musical standpoint, the character of the repetition of the (E D B) fragment is ritualistic. With the pitch E as the point of departure and return, melody in the opening passage of *The Wedding* consists of E, D, and B, with F# sounded as a grace note to the D. The confinement of melody to these three or four pitches extends to subsequent restatements of this material. Within each of the latter, returns to E are always preceded by the D. At the same time, D, succeeded by E in this fashion, is always inflected by the grace note F#, and is always doubled and accented by Pianos I and III and the xylophone.

Successive taps on the cymbal (wooden mallet) are no less systematic (again, see example 5.1). The time-spans between these taps number seven, six, five, four, three, and two eighth-note beats, respectively, with each span marked by the reduction of a single beat. In this way, the pattern of repetition in the cymbal unfolds as a separate layer, independently of the repetition in the vocal and instrumental parts. A large-scale stratification may be inferred, the sort of polyrhythmic layering alluded to in earlier chapters.

Crucially, too, the vocal and instrumental parts in this opening passage are never exchanged in an imitative dialogue, but are fixed in register as well as in part. No "conversation" may be detected on the part of the (E D B) motive, no imitative interaction between the parts or instruments. Nor are there any transpositions in subsequent restatements of this passage.

Indeed, the system, hardness, and inertness identified with much of Stravinsky's music can seem to have reached an early prime in these opening bars of *The Wedding*. From start to finish, harmony or vertical coincidence is fixed with little or no sense of movement or progress. Putting aside the pitchless taps on the cymbal (the only source here of a form of stratification), harmony midway through this passage is little different from what it is at the beginning or at the conclusion.

More to the point, the small motive D-E in the soprano (see the brackets in example 5.2) always falls over the bar line. Irrespective of the notated irregularity, D-E always assumes the same metrical alignment. Hence, the score would seem to latch on to a fixed element or constancy, here in the form of the pervasive D-E segment. In addition, E, as the registrally fixed pitch of departure and return, always falls on the first beats of the shifting bar lines.

Indeed, as can readily be seen, the notated irregularity of block A is in large part determined by these metrically fixed alignments. The shifting bar lines seek, at least in part, to preserve fixed or parallel alignments for D-E and the single pitch E.

At the same time, however, all is not as it might at first appear. Against the intensely static implications of the (E D B) melody in the soprano solo, a number of forces do shift flexibly. As Stravinsky's rapidly changing bar lines make clear, returns to E as the point of departure are irregularly spaced, underscored not only by the octave doublings accompanying the initial D of the D-E motive (in Pianos I and III), but also by a punctuating D in the xylophone.

In turn, when set against an inferred metrical periodicity, the irregularity of the spans between repeats of the D-E segments will mean that the latter will be *displaced*. As the 1-2-3 brackets affixed to the staves in example 5.1 indicate, a 3/8 meter may be inferred from the D-E motive of the opening two measures and imposed on the block as a whole.

In the opening two measures of *The Wedding*, the stressed D-E unit assumes its over-the-barline, upbeat-downbeat placement. But subsequent repeats contradict this identity. In the 3/8 barring of example 5.1, the D in this succession falls on the second at m.3, and then on the first beat m.6. Hence a patterned cycle of displacement is revealed. The D of the D-E motive is introduced on the third beat, and is subsequently displaced to the second and first beats, and then, in the completion of the cycle, is displaced yet another notch back to the original third beat. At this point, D-E resumes its original alignment in the final bars of the block. At the same time, the 3/8 meter emerges on target with the notated irregularity. The two conflicting meters are aligned as block A draws to a close. This is likely to intensify the listener's feel of the 3/8 meter, along with the displacements.

The Wedding's "melodic inventions"

The melodic material of *The Wedding* consists typically not of melodies or themes, properly speaking, but of fragments or motives. Numbering two to five pitches, these fragments are open-ended and without cadential expression, inviting the immediate and often continuous repetition encountered already in the opening passage of the first tableau. At the same time, open-endedness is tied to a diatonicism that it distinctly modal and often Dorian, with many of the fragments outlining Dorian tetrachords. Typical are the minor-third gaps that pervade these tetrachords; the D-B gap in (E D B), for example, which lacks a C#.

In fact, when gapped or incomplete in this fashion, the Dorian tetrachord assumes the earmarks of what Arnold Schoenberg might have called a melodic cell or "basic motive." Inversions surface in this light, that is, as departures from the parent or untransformed version. Minor-third gaps pervade lengthier segments as well, with *The Wedding* acquiring a *pentatonic* character. Subject to a repetition which is often relentless, the gaps are made all the more conspicuous. The repetition intensifies the sense of what is being omitted—namely, semitones and their potential for creating a sense of movement by way of the leading-tone function. While the reduction in intervals would have made for a somewhat static framework in any case, the particular gaps in question intensify the archaic or "primitive" character of the folk element. Many of the melodic characteristics of *The Wedding* may be attributed to Russian folk music or church music. As transcribed by the composer in 1909, appearances of a borrowed folk song in the fourth tableau, "Ne vesyolaya da komtan'itsa" (Not a Merry Company"), are exceptional in *The Wedding*. They are the only instances in which a borrowed melody is quoted in its entirety.

More typical of the melodic invention in *The Wedding* is the D-E motive of the opening block (again, see example 5.1). It is not a melody, strictly speaking, but a segment of a segment, the closing figure of (E D B). Fragments of this kind are not traceable to specific sources, but are folk-like rather than folk-derived. They are products not of borrowing but of *simulation* ("fabrication," as Stravinsky described it). Many are "faithful and clever imitations of folk songs," to follow Bela Bartok's early account of Stravinsky's methods. And this applies not only to *The Wedding*, but to other late Russian-period works as well, including the *Three Pieces for String Quartet* (1914), *Renard* (1916), *The Soldier's Tale* (1918), and the *Symphonies of Wind Instruments* (1920).

In sum, Stravinsky's uniquely designed late Russian-period style was served often enough not by the genuine article, but by more intrinsically or "organically" developed material—melodic parts whose origins lay more immediately with the compositional processes at hand. Such parts were the product of a musical consciousness steeped in Russian folk idioms, to be sure, but perhaps more particularly to the uses to which those idioms could be put, the ways in which they could be made to serve rhythmic and metrical practices already fully a part of Stravinsky's style. And the further the composer traveled from his point of departure in the form of the three early ballets (*The Firebird, Petrushka,* and *The Rite of Spring*), the more problematic the explicit borrowing of authentic folk songs and the process of assimilation appear to have been. "If any of these [Russian-period] pieces *sounds* like aboriginal folk music," Stravinsky would later remark, "it may be because my powers of fabrication were able to tap some unconscious 'folk' memory."[4]

In his lengthy polemic against "folkloristic symphonies," Schoenberg argued against the use of borrowed folk or popular material, suggesting that such material could never be assimilated properly by the constructed artwork.[5] In Schoenberg's view, the two sides of this equation could not be made to cohere. And the problem lay with the mode of conception. Borrowed folk melodies were conceived outside the compositional process. They came whole and readymade, implying not some further development, but qualities that were capable of being appreciated and savored for what they already were. An aesthetic purpose had been realized in full, in other words, and short of merely repeating that purpose in various settings or arrangements, little could be added.

In effect, bits and pieces of a borrowed folk melody could not be chiseled off and submitted to a developing variation, the traditional and Classical means by which, according to Schoenberg, motivic parts were worked into the body of a work and made whole and organic, individual and contextual. And attempts to work them in this way, to treat them as if they had in fact sprung from the compositional process itself, were doomed to failure. They could not but lead to an acute form of artificiality, something forced and labored. And the character of the borrowed material, which had in all likelihood prompted the borrowing in the first place, would be lost in the process.

But this argument fails where Stravinsky's methods are considered more specifically. The "folkloristic" in pieces such as *The Wedding* and *Renard* has far less to do with the incorporation of Russian folk songs borrowed whole than with the manipulation of short, open-ended fragments traceable often enough to Stravinsky's "powers of fabrication." This is not to deny the few instances of direct and explicit borrowing, but only to suggest that such borrowing figured as but one of the many ways in which the folk element was exploited.

Indeed, the issue of melody was often a sensitive and complicated one for Stravinsky. In the small-scale cutting and pasting of fragments, another sort of melody was required, different in kind from that which had characterized the music of his predecessors. Greater pliancy was needed—the ability of a melody to submit to the processes of division, repetition, and metrical displacement detailed here and in previous chapters. And what critics condemned early on as a "lack of melody" in Stravinsky's music can therefore be described more accurately as the absence of a particular kind of melody, the sorts of themes or "beautiful melodies" made famous in the music of his compatriots, composers such as Pyotr Tchaikovsky and Sergei Rachmaninoff.

A certain ambiguity is thus likely to attach itself to the above assertion regarding the folk or church-related origins of much of the melodic content of *The Wedding*. There are cases of direct borrowing, to be sure, cases traceable at least in part to authentic sources. Yet much of the material of *The Wedding* seems to have been conceived in the manner indicated by the composer, that is, as a form of improvisation *a la manière de*, a simulation in which, from the start of the compositional process, bits and pieces of folk music, tapped sometimes from the composer's "unconscious folk memory," meshed with the ways and means of his own stylistic devices. And from what we know of the approach, it could not have differed all that much from the ways in which neoclassical works were formed. Beneath the surface of these two large-scale orientations, the Russian folk models that had served the earlier Russian period were replaced by the Baroque and Classical materials that would serve the later neoclassical one.

6. The Swiss Years (II): *Renard* (1916)

A burlesque about the fox, the cock, the cat, and the goat, to be sung and played on stage. 2 solo tenors, 2 solo basses; percussion, timpani, cimbalom. Dedicated to Princess Edmond de Polignac. First performance, Ballets Russes, Paris Opera, Paris, May 18, 1922.

In September 1915, Stravinsky and his family moved from Clarens to Morges, near Lausanne, settling first in a rental and then, a year or so later, on the second floor of the Maison Bornand, a *pension* not far from the center of town. Swiss writers and musicians now figured among his closest friends. They included Charles-Albert Cingria, a writer and composer, and the conductor Ernest Ansermet, to whom Stravinsky dedicated his *Three Pieces for String Quartet*. Ansermet was followed by the Swiss novelist C. F. Ramuz, who in turn introduced him to the artist René Auberjonois. The latter three would play pivotal roles in the conception and eventual production of *The Soldier's Tale*.

First to be realized was *Renard*, however. This was the "burlesque" for which, beginning sometime in the fall of 1915, *The Wedding* was set aside for about seven months. Slighter and less celebrated than *The Wedding*, *Renard* is the bearer of much extraordinary music all the same. Its composition began with the setting of the verses of a single folk tale, "The Cat, the Cock, and the Fox." Listed as No.38 in Alexander Afanasyev's vast anthology of Russian folklore, *Russian Fairy Tales*, the title was originally *Renard*'s as well. As the piece progressed, however, Stravinsky was soon adding, compiling, and conflating folk tales and fragments of texts just as he had earlier with the verses of the Kireyevsky volume when working on *The Wedding*. The result, a conflation of barnyard scenes, was a burlesque conceived in "gentle mockery and fun," as he once described it.[1]

Remarkably, *Renard* contains no direct borrowings of Russian folk tunes. Its "authentic" music is entirely Stravinsky's own, as is, for that matter, the genre itself, a unique hybrid of folk play, *divertissement*, and ballet. The performance instructions bear this out. The composer had intended to recreate the atmosphere of a street performance, with itinerant players occupying an impromptu space shared with the audience: "The play is acted by clowns, dancers, or acrobats, preferably on a trestle stage placed in front of the orchestra. If performed in a theatre it should be played in front of the curtain." The scenario opens with a cock strutting about on a perch, eyeing a fox (Renard) with empty heroics. Disguised in various ways, Renard manages to capture his prey, only to lose him to a cat and goat. The dramatic action is repeated, with the cock caught and saved a second time.

"Phonetic sonority of the words and syllables"

Entrusted with the French translation of *Renard*'s text was Ramuz, who would later publish a short memoir of his experiences with the composer, *Souvenirs sur Igor Strawinsky* (1929). Included in his recollections is a description of his method of approach with Stravinsky:

> We met almost every day in the blue room overlooking the garden; we were among the drums, the timpani, the bass drums, every kind of bashing instrument (or percussion, to use the official term), to which had been recently been added the cimbalom. I had a sheet of paper, a pencil. Stravinsky read me the Russian text verse by verse, taking care each time to count the number of syllables in each verse, which I would write down in the margin of my paper;

then we made the translation, that is, Stravinsky translated the text for me word for word. It was a word-for-word so literal as to be often quite incomprehensible, but with an inspired (nonlogical) imagery, meetings of words whose freshness was all the greater for lacking any (logical) sense.

In matters of text-setting generally during the Swiss years, Stravinsky was drawn to the special musical-rhythmic qualities of Russian folk verse. Eager to exploit these qualities in a music of his own, his sketches and notebooks became infused with bits of texts besmirched with prosody marks. Indeed, so immersed was he for a time in the sound, character, and rhythm of this poetry that the librettos of both *The Wedding* and *Renard*, although pieced together from texts derived from the Kireyevsky and Afanasyev collections, contain much that is undoubtedly his. At work on both librettos, he began to invent and interpolate onomatopoeic nonsense words of his own.

More specifically, it was the "phonetic sonority of the words and syllables" that attracted him; sound sense rather than word sense. His attention was drawn, "his musical saliva was set in motion," by the sounds and rhythms of the syllables.

Momentous was a discovery of his during the early days of the Swiss period. Late in 1914, Stravinsky was struck by a feature peculiar to Russian folk verse: when sung, the accents of the spoken verse are often ignored. A recollection of this discovery, one of the most "rejoicing" of his life, was later included in *Expositions and Developments*:

> One important characteristic of Russian popular verse is that the accents of the spoken verse are ignored when the verse is sung. The recognition of the musical possibilities inherent in this fact was one of the most rejoicing discoveries of my life; I was like a man who suddenly finds that his finger can be bent from the second joint as well as the first. We all know parlor games in which the same

sentence can be made to mean something different when the different words are emphasized.[2]

In *Renard*, the syllable-sounds within the word itself, as well as the emphasis of the word in the sentence, are so treated. *Renard* is phoneme music, and phonemes are untranslatable.

A revelation, then, the discovery of this discrepancy in the pronunciation of popular Russian verse. The idea must surely have dawned on the composer that here, in this quaint, "backwoods" oddity of Russian folk poetry, was a capability akin to that which he had already pursued in musical rhythm and meter. In this freeing of the syllabification from fixed practice by varying not only the emphasis of words within a sentence, but also the manner in which the syllables were pronounced, he had stumbled on a flexible coordination which, put to his own use, could complement the metrical displacement of repeated fragments and chords that were already inextricably a part of his musical language. He could pursue a varied accentuation that was relatively indifferent to the musical component, or he could vary a verbal accent in accord with some variance in metrical placement. The possibilities must have seemed infinite. For no longer were the metrical displacements of repeated themes and fragments in his music helplessly at the mercy of a fixed practice in verbal accentuation. His fingers could be bent "from the second joint as well as from the first."

It is significant, too, that this capability realized in popular Russian verse was never abandoned during the neoclassical and serial eras. His native tongue no longer of practical use, Stravinsky was not to relent as he turned first to Latin in *Oedipus Rex* (1927), to French and English, and finally to Hebrew in one of his late serial conceptions, *Abraham and Isaac* (1963). Setting his "musical saliva in motion," the "*sounds*" of the syllables remained for him the central focus. Treated as phonetic material, the text could be "dissected" at will.

And so Stravinsky's musical imagination was stirred less by

meaning or imagery than by "phonetic sonority." To such an extent did this prove to be the case, that, late in life, he would come to dislike Ramuz's French translations of his early Russian librettos, preferring to hear this music "in Russian or not at all." In accentuation and timbre, the syllables and their sounds were too integral a part of the musical conception.

Cimbalom enters the scene

The vocal complement of *Renard* consists of two solo tenors and two basses, while its chamber "orchestra of soloists" included a cimbalom, an instrument Stravinsky had discovered in a bar in Geneva. So entirely enamored did he become with the resonant and somewhat raucous sound of this instrument, that he purchased one and had it installed in his studio, an addition to the expanding facilities of his "musical pantry." Stravinsky soon learned how to play it as well, composing much of *Renard* "on" the cimbalom, just as he would continue to compose the bulk of his music at the piano. What attracted his attention at the time was the cimbalom's approximation in sound to that of the ancient, string-plucked Russian gusli, which had inspired some of the early verses of *Renard's* libretto. So soft and delicate was the gusli's plucked sonority, however, that its replacement by the cimbalom soon proved necessary. (The gusli was very nearly extinct as well.) Stravinsky was partial to wooden sticks that lit up the glittering delicacy of the cimbalom's hammered sound like the crackling of ice cubes, the sound becoming "as compact as billiard balls." In Paris during the neoclassical years, he added a cimbalom to his Pleyel studio, where he continued to tune and tinker with it on a daily basis.

Another discovery of Stravinsky's during these Swiss years was American jazz or ragtime, live performances of which had reached Paris before the war. Stephen Walsh suspects the composer of having heard some of these early renditions, echoing forth from cafes, dance halls, and American bars. Stravinsky's appetite for the idiom was further whetted when, in early 1916, Ansermet returned from a tour with the Ballets Russes in the United States with a pile of sheet scores. Within a year or so Stravinsky was composing his own *Ragtime* (1917-18) for eleven instruments, which included a cimbalom. In 1919 he improvised and composed a short work, *Piano-Rag-Music*.

What may have caught the composer's attention at the time were not only the dotted rhythms and syncopations of the ragtime style, but also the fact that the syncopations were often tied to metrical displacements, slight shifts in the metrical alignment of repeated motives. Displacement of this kind, mentioned already in our discussion of the Finale of the *Firebird* and *The Wedding*, had by the time of *Renard* become a *style characteristic* of Stravinsky's, one that would eventually be transcending the familiar three stylistic periods. Indeed, as should by now be apparent, the characteristic can be held responsible for much of the rhythmic vitality in Stravinsky's music, a matter to which we will be turning at greater length in Chapter 8.

7. The Swiss Years (III): *The Soldier's Tale* (1918)

Ideas for *The Soldier's Tale*, a kind of a *théâtre ambulant*, as Stravinsky described it—music with an accompanying play that could be hustled quickly from one Swiss town to the next—began to develop in early 1918. Partly in response to the economic pressures of WWI, Stravinsky and Ramuz decided to stage it in September. The forces required for its performance included three narrators, two actors, a dancer, and seven instrumentalists. Following the example of *Renard*, and in the tradition of itinerant theater, all players were assigned to the stage for the entire performance. New, however, was the relationship between the music and the text. The music was conceived as a "suite" of pieces that could be performed independently of the libretto.

As with *Renard*, too, the libretto was drawn from Afanasyev's anthology, this time almost exclusively from No.154, "The Runaway Soldier and the Devil." It unfolds in a strictly narrative fashion and without the textual conflations of *The Wedding* and *Renard*. And instead of being set to music, the text was designed to be read above or between the individual pieces. Stravinsky and Ramuz had hoped to skirt the difficulties of translation, the need more specifically for a syllable-by-syllable translation from Russian.

The hope, too, had been that both the story and the direct manner of its presentation would attract an international and potentially profitable audience. The subject matter itself, a somewhat skewed version of the Faust legend, was universally known. Briefly, a soldier falls prey to the devil, who, in a pattern of repetition characteristic of Russian folk tales, appears variously as a cattle merchant, an old woman, a violin virtuoso, and finally in his true form (with tail and pointed ears). The content of the story itself was made more flexible. Regional linguistics, along with the style of soldier's uniform, could be adjusted to the circumstances of local custom.

To quote from Maureen Carr's study of the sketches, "It was as though the collaborators had woven two strands, the spoken text and the music; each would take turns in coming to the forefront".[1] Yet the independence of the music in *The Soldier's Tale* proved problematic from a theatrical standpoint. Ansermet, who conducted the first performance at the Théâtre Municipal in Lausanne on September 28, 1918, singled out the music as the featured player in the collaboration. "The score of *The Soldier's Tale* is really absolute music," he explained, "the purely musical interest of which remains in tact when it is detached from the other elements".[2]

Alas, the original conception and promise of *The Soldier's Tale* as a touring piece was never realized. Directly following the premiere, subsequent performances in Lausanne, Zurich, and Geneva were canceled owing to the epidemic of Spanish influenza that had spread through parts of Europe. Performances had to be called off due to illness on the part of the actors and musicians, while, elsewhere, theaters were closed by the municipal authorities. (The flu epidemic of 1918, the deadliest pandemic in human history, killed at least 50 million people, primarily in Europe and Asia.)

A shortened version of *The Soldier's Tale* for clarinet, violin, and piano (music only) was first performed in Lausanne on November 8, 1919. A lengthier "concert suite" followed in 1920. But much is necessarily lost in these transcriptions: apart from the play and its libretto, various sections, and their instrumentations. And it is the whole of *The Soldier's Tale* that contains some of Stravinsky's greatest music, not stray parts thereof. To an extent far greater than Ansermet was willing to admit, the music and the remarkable effect it can have on the listener is timed and conditioned by the narrative, however dated or otherwise flawed might the text and its enactment be from any number of perspectives. Indeed, from the start, the music of *The Soldier's Tale* has been handicapped (disadvantaged) by the literary and dramatic circumstances of its conception.

This is not to imply that the music could not have been inspired by those circumstances. That is a separate issue, however. If the music is to achieve its maximum effect, then it cannot be separated or "freed" from its text.

"Merging of divergent types of music"

For the most part, *The Soldier's Tale* falls easily within the parameters of the composer's late Russian-period style. Ostinatos abound, and serve not only as a barrier to harmonic progression, but also as a backdrop for the shifts in the metrical alignment of the repeated fragments and chords. (The rapidly shifting bar lines in the score may be felt as accents by the listener, syncopations against a continuing meter, with the latter enforced by a basso ostinato, often pizzicato in the double bass.) Apart from the popular verse on which *The Soldier's Tale* is based, the melodic invention is short and repetitive, just as it is in *The Wedding* and *Renard*. Like these previous works, too, there are few—if any—direct borrowings of authentic Russian folk songs. The "authentic" music is nearly entirely Stravinsky's own.

The music to Scene II, as poignant an episode as Stravinsky ever penned, accompanies the Soldier's sorrowful contemplation of his plight. Featured is a modal/diatonic base that is inflected chromatically by the intervention of octatonic intervals. This happens in a manner entirely reminiscent of *The Wedding* and *Renard*.

But there are neoclassical peculiarities as well. The marching tune of the opening "Soldier's March" implies the D-major scale (especially at rehearsal no. 5). Following condensed repeats of the music to Scenes I and II, the "Royal March" and its reference to B-flat major is followed by three stylized dances (or dance "portraits", as Stravinsky called them), "Tango," "Waltz," and "Ragtime". The latter are succeeded by two chorales, "Little" and "Great," but *pseudo* in that they, too, are stylized as ritual, being "portraits" or snapshots of the authentic German-Protestant model.

In sum, *The Soldier's Tale* is something of a crossroads piece. While its initial sections are distinctly Russian, later ones encompass peculiarities already very much a part of neoclassicism. And so we detect a hint of a Stravinsky increasingly restless within the confines of his uniquely fashioned Russian musical thought, increasingly eager to strike out from this terrain. And this need not be surprising, for he had already composed somewhat similarly in 1915. Introducing the "Polka" of his *Eight Easy Pieces* for piano duet to Diaghilev and the Italian composer Alfredo Casella in February of 1915, he was aware, as he later recalled, that "a new path had been indicated," that "neoclassicism of a sort" had been born. And the "suggestion" that was to lead to the ballet *Pucinella* (1920)—Stravinsky's first full-scale neoclassical ordeal—lay just around the corner.

And then there is the jazz idiom, one with which Stravinsky had familiarized himself through sheet music provided by his friend Ansermet, and whose impact, apart from the "Ragtime" itself, may be felt in the jazz-like instrumental grouping of small ensemble and percussion. (Minus the saxophone, however. Stravinsky disliked its heavy, swelling vibrato, and opted for the bassoon instead.) The jazz element points in turn to an eclectic strain in *The Soldier's Tale* and in Stravinsky's music generally, to the manner in which a confrontation of opposites is posed, resulting in an awkward, disjointed kind of incongruity. For example: *Petrushka's* blend of authentic Russian folk melodies and contemporary chansons. Or the fact that "traces of blues and boogie-woogie" should be found in some of Stravinsky's most "serious" ventures, including the "pas d'action" and "pas de deux" of the neoclassical ballet *Orpheus* (1947). Or that a piece like *Oedipus Rex* (1928), high neoclassicism at its highest and most austere, should likewise partake of this freakish, eclectic strain. Much of *Oedipus* is a "fusion of widely divergent types of music".[3]

And this merging of "divergent types of music" is as much a part of *The Soldier's Tale* as it was of *Petrushka*, and would be of *Oedipus, Orpheus,* and *Agon*. The marching tunes of the opening "March" of *The Soldier's Tale* are related to what the English music critic Wilfrid Mellers has called "clichés common to European art music".[4] They are followed by the forlorn "sigh" of Scene II, and then by a pompous "Royal March" composed of "snippets of Italian opera" and "corny Spanish figurations." The latter is followed by the burlesque of the three contemporary dances, dances followed in turn by the two stylized "snapshots" of a German-Protestant chorale.

And all this is transmitted by an ensemble with percussion that closely resembles a jazz band from New Orleans. Of course, as in *Petrushka* and later in *Oedipus*, a unity is forged. From this raw material, a new reality emerges, something, again, peculiarly Stravinsky's own. But we are at the same time not unmindful of how strange must this unity have seemed in 1918; indeed, in the wake of the post-romantic era, how outlandish a concoction to all serious musicians and audiences. (The first-night audience in Lausanne was indeed baffled by *The Soldier's Tale*. Although courteous, the critics on the morning after were bewildered by the music and its underlying aesthetics.)

Then, too, linked to *The Soldier's Tale* as a crossroads piece—or as an eclectic excursion—is its instrumental compression. For this work marks Stravinsky's final break with the 19th-century "Russian orchestral school" in which he had been "fostered," and seals, at the same time, the raw "solo-instrumental style" toward which his invention had been inclining since 1914. It was the "discovery of American jazz" (the sound of jazz, its small ensemble and percussion), along with the experience of *The Soldier's Tale*, that ultimately sealed the instrumental fate of *The Wedding*. For the preoccupation with percussion here dramatically reduced the earlier cloaks in which *The Wedding* had been conceived, leading in 1918-19 to the penultimate version for two cimbaloms, harmonium, pianolas, percussion (requiring five players), and then to the final "perfectly homogeneous, perfectly impersonal, and perfectly mechanical" settlement for four pianos and percussion in 1923.

But the "master orchestrator" who would seem to lurk with such certainty behind conceptions like *Petrushka* and *The Soldier's Tale*, the composer who always "orchestrated while he composed," the inventor of novel instrumental blends with an uncanny feeling for the sound capabilities of individuals—this "master" has drawn unexpected criticism. With particular reference to *The Soldier's Tale*, this sensitivity has been viewed by critics like Pierre Boulez as a fetish, a tyrannical "tic" flexed as an "end in itself" and at the expense of musical substance (a substance which, while scintillating in instrumental garb, might alarm by its poverty when transcribed by the piano).

No doubt, Stravinsky would have responded to such criticism as he had when questioned about his "manners" in *Oedipus*: that it was impossible for him to separate the manner of saying something from what was said, that "the manner of saying and the thing said are, for me, the same." And, indeed, given the nature of this intimacy, this felt inseparability of substance from instrumental transmission, from "the physical conditions of sound emission," Boulez's argument seems naïve. For even if the naked substance of Stravinsky's music (whatever that can mean, given this intimacy) presupposed instrumental perception of a kind quite different from that experienced by a composer like Webern, can this legitimately constitute grounds for reproach? Assuming that Stravinsky was no mere predator of "effect"? Assuming that he did in fact have something to say in pieces like *The Soldier's Tale*?

One is far more apt to marvel at the physical aspect of Stravinsky's musicality, the magnificent non-abstractness of his methods, the application of this extraordinary intimacy. Thus, his "discovery of American jazz" led him to purchase the instruments at a store in Lausanne and to play them as he composed. By the end of 1918, his studio in Morges bulged with a "cuisine" of percussion instruments, a cimbalom, a harmonium, and a pianola. "I had packed all of the instruments into my little musical pantry and learned to play all of them myself, spending as much time practicing them, in fact, and tinkering with and tuning the cimbalom, as I did composing ....

Risky as my memory is, too, I am certain of the position of each of the instruments of this little orchestra in my room, which must be because my acoustical reality ... is part of my biological reality."[5]

But what ultimately astonishes most about Stravinsky's instrumental invention are the stunning limitations imposed from one context to the next, the restraint pursued, the always apparent and enviable ability "to make due." Except perhaps for some early pieces such as the *Scherzo fantastique* and *Fireworks*, this invention is distinguished not by a taste for the exotic, extravagant, or ostentatious, but by these limited courses of action; in addition to a truly remarkable diversity and ingenuity in instrumental grouping (so evident in *The Soldier's Tale* and in a piece such as *Agon*), the persuasive manner in which selective ensembles persevere, the restrictions that seem always to have been a necessary preamble to composition. These are scarcely the symptoms of an orchestral playboy, but bespeak a rare and miraculous fluency—a "sixth sense."

8. Stravinsky the Rhythmic Genius

When I was nine my parents gave me a piano mistress. I very quickly learned to read music, and, as the result of reading, soon had a longing to improvise, a pursuit to which I devoted myself, and which for a long time was my favorite occupation .... I must say that my constant work at improvisation was not absolutely fruitless; for, on the one hand, it contributed to my better knowledge of the piano, and, on the other, it sowed the seed of musical ideas. [Igor Stravinsky, *An Autobiography*]

Often Stravinsky came early to the theatre before a rehearsal began [*The Firebird*, 1910] in order to play for me over and over again some specifically difficult passage .... It was interesting to watch him at the piano. His body seemed to vibrate with his own rhythm; punctuating staccatos with his head, he made the pattern of his music forcibly clear to me, more so than the counting of bars would have been. That rhythm lives in, at times took possession of, his body became evident to me as I watched him through the familiar intercourse of the following years. [Tamara Karsavina, "A Recollection of Stravinsky".]

I stood behind him [December, 1947] and watched the short, nervous fingers scour the keyboard .... His neck, his head, his whole body accentuated the ingenious rhythmical design of the music by spasm-like bobs and jerks. He grunted, he hummed, and occasionally stopped to make an aside .... [Nicolas Nabokov, "Christmas with Stravinsky".]

A real composer is not one who plays first on the piano and writes down what he has played .... A real composer conceives his ideas, his entire music, in his mind, in his imagination, and does not need an instrument. [*Arnold Schoenberg Letters*, ed. Edwin Stein.]

We apprehend and acknowledge the *physical* nature and appearance of Stravinsky and his music. "I am no mystic," he conceded in *Retrospectives and Conclusions*. "I need to touch music as well as to think it, which is why I have always lived next to a piano". And so, the piano was never strictly a pianist's piano, even if it might occasionally be necessary to indulge, if not as a way of making a living, then as a way of bringing his performance intentions to light.

But, neither, evidently, was the composer's use of the piano restricted to a constant tuning of the ear, a constant testing "measure by measure." The piano appears first and foremost to have serviced an instinctual, biological need to be physically at one with music, to be physically engaged with its invention and expression. We see that, in contrast to Arnold Schoenberg's bleak proposal, to the effect that "a real composer conceives his entire music in his mind, in his imagination, and does not need an instrument" (see above), improvisation was not to be belittled or discredited: "fingers are great inspirers," wrote Stravinsky in his *Autobiography* (as quoted already); in contact with a musical instrument, [they] often give birth to subconscious ideas which might otherwise never come to life."

Indeed, during and following Stravinsky's cautious adoption of serial techniques during the 1950s and 60s, composition continued at the piano (the reliance may have intensified), and was preceded, as always, by "relating intervals rhythmically," an "exploration of possibilities always conducted at the piano".[1] The preference for a muted instrument was no contradiction. Neutralizing the piano, the muting removed (in most cases) some of its distractive "pianism," and helped keep the ear fastened to an instrumental hearing. (Or so we surmise. For Stravinsky orchestrated while he composed. And it is often the case that, when dealing with a musical score away from the piano, one's contextual and instrumental bearings are disrupted with any sudden injection of "pianism." But the muted piano may also have allayed Stravinsky's dread of eavesdropping.)

And the early rehearsals and auditions with Tamara Karsavina, who first danced the role of the Firebird in 1910, and much later with Nicolas Nabokov at Christmas time in 1947; trance-like gruntings, hummings, and "spasm-like bobs and jerks." Musical invention and expression appear for Stravinsky to have been uncompromisingly involuntary and impulsive–inward, passionate, and utterly subjective inclinations. Hence, too, inscrutable. Stravinsky shied away from systematic "explanation," felt ill at ease, and often annoyed with conscious analytic-theoretical reckoning. If not debased or defrauded by verbal (metaphorical) description, the message was trivialized by formal, explanatory hardware.

Of course, analysis might be pursued in response to immediate, urgently felt, creative needs. But a compulsion to regurgitate digested food stuffs, to systematically retrace one's steps as a kind of semi-autonomous intellectual activity–this appears to have been acutely alien to this mentality, perhaps a waste of time, a real bore. "I care less about my 'works' than about composing," he noted.

But perhaps not even a bore, a form of introspection that might ruinously distract the innate taste buds, the cherished certainty of the immediate, subjective response; perhaps, too often, misguidance, a misunderstanding of the artistic endeavor and its special appeal. Present-day thinkers to the contrary, the perceptual-conceptual, practice-theory, sensual-intellectual, innate-learned, doer-thinker dichotomies remained for Stravinsky meaningful distinctions. Stravinsky would admit that "we certainly love *talking* conceptually," but "the composer works through a perceptual, not a conceptual, process."[2]

Stravinsky fancied himself a "natural," then, an instinctual and self-disciplined composer; a "doer," never "mirror struck" by his mental functions. ("My interest passes entirely to the object, the thing made.") And so it is to be supposed that he would not have sensed the urgency of the critic's plea for a continuing dialogue, for inside conceptual or descriptive assistance. Stravinsky might have countered that such "assistance" is as apt to confuse or mislead as it is to illuminate. "I do not see any means of explaining why I have chosen a certain note if whoever hears it does not already know why when he hears it".[3]

Even if the benefits of analysis and theory lay less in formal "explanation" or "justification" (as he implies), than in the process itself, in the seeking to better hear and understand, and in the attempt to bring oneself closer to the music (a process in which the conceptual and perceptual boundaries cannot even be felt to overlap, but are meshed and indistinguishable), then, just possibly, such pedagogical pursuits were the business of interested parties. Although he might occasionally intervene to avert or correct gross distortions, as an interpreter or observer, his works could not be salvaged or made more credible by analysis, by inside conceptual or descriptive assistance, however rigorous, ingenious, or well-intentioned.

Metrical displacement and parallelism

To what might the pronounced physicality of Stravinsky's engagement with music be attributed? What might have prompted the composer's head "to punctuate the staccatos," his body to accentuate "the ingenious rhythmical design of the music by spasm-like bobs and jerks?" Like so much that surrounds his music and the effect it can have on the listener, these behaviors can be traced in part to rhythmic phenomena, more specifically, to what we have been calling *metrical displacement*.

When a motive or short melodic fragment is repeated and shifted from, say, the upbeat to the downbeat of a measure, the listener's expectations of *metrical parallelism*–expectations that the fragment will be repeated at the same (or *parallel*) location vis-à-vis the bar line–are frustrated. In turn, upsetting the listener's expectations in this regard can result in challenging and even disrupting her metrical bearings. This is because, in the listener's mind, parallelism can play an essential role in the actual establishment and continuing confirmation of a meter.

For a straightforward case in point, see, in example 8.1a, b, c, and d, the series of metrical displacements of the short melodic fragment, A-D-C-D. (Singled out in these examples is the horn fragment in the lengthy stratification at rehearsal nos.67-71 in *The Rite of Spring*.) The spans between successive repeats of the A-D-C-D fragment are uneven and sometimes irregular, causing it ultimately to fall on all four quarter-note beats of the 4/4 measure. Introduced on the fourth quarter-note beat in example 8.1a, the fragment is shifted to the downbeat in example 8.1b. In examples 8.1c and d, the fragment falls on the third and second beats, respectively. Since the main beat for the listener is likely to be the half-note beat at 83 beats per minute, the sensation of falling on and off of it is likely to be paramount. The half-note beat intersects with the first and third quarter-note beats of the 4/4 bar line. Falling off the half-note beat will mean falling on the second and third quarter-note beats.

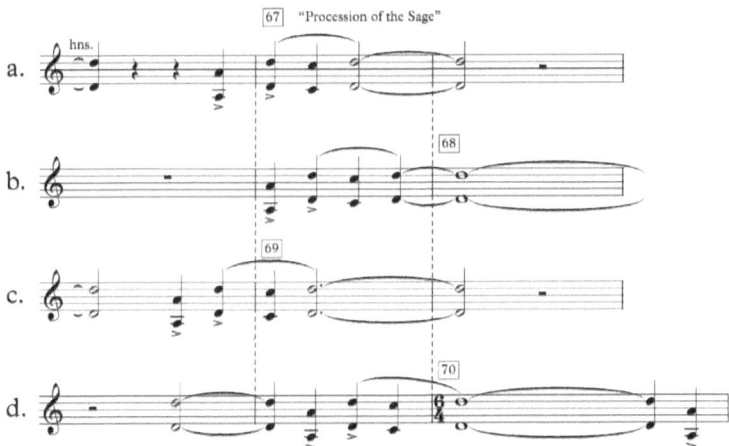

EXAMPLE 8.1a, b, c, and d: *The Rite of Spring*, "Ritual of the Rival Tribes," "Procession of the Sage," stratification; metrical displacement of horn fragment

Stravinsky the Rhythmic Genius | 93

Stravinsky's notation in examples 8.1a, b, c, and d is *conservative*, meaning that a steady meter is applied, allowing the successive displacements of the A-D-C-D fragment to be exposed to the eye. And the assumption is that the listener will respond accordingly—that is, *conservatively*. The meter will be sustained (*conserved*), allowing the successive displacements to be heard as written.

This is scarcely the whole of it, however. The shifts in the metrical alignment of the A-D-C-D fragment are highlighted by what does *not* change, namely, *everything else*. Pitch, register, and instrumentation are held constant as the vertical alignment of the fragment shifts in relation to the meter. (Even the articulation of A-D-C-D, with the pitches A and D accented and D-C-D slurred, is fixed from one displaced repeat to the next.) Features other than alignment are retained in order that alignment itself (and its shifts) might be set in relief. The literalism of the repetition acts as a foil in this respect.

Yet the literal character of the repetition of A-D-C-D acts as *counterforce*, too, a way of referring the listener *back* to the fragment's original placement. With all other features of the motive retained, the expectation is that its original alignment off the half-note beat and on the fourth quarter-note beat of the bar line will be repeated as well. And the more that is repeated literally, the more fully aroused are these conflicting expectations of metrical parallelism likely to be.

Here the implications for the listener are fiendish. To repeat the fragment literally and without variation so as to highlight and expose its metrical displacement is to undermine that displacement at the same time. It is to raise a conflicting signal of metrical parallelism. Typically, and with varying degrees of intensity, listeners are caught off guard by this. Unable to commit themselves initially to a reading of displacement or to one of metrical parallelism, they are apt to lose their metrical bearings. And the metrical disruption does not have to do with one or the other of these two signals, but with their *conflict*, with the fact that there is insufficient evidence for an easy, automatic ruling in favor of one or the other. In this way, the two forces of displacement and parallelism are irreconcilable. The listener can adapt to one and experience the other as a kind of challenge, but he cannot attend to both simultaneously.

In the *radical* alternative to the conservative readings discussed above, the bar line would shift in order that the repetition of the A-D-C-D fragment might be aligned in a parallel fashion. Both the fragment's initial appearance and its subsequent repetition would fall on the fourth quarter-note beat of the bar line, with the passage read *radically*. And much of the motivation for the notated metrical irregularity in Stravinsky's music may be traced accordingly—that is, to attempts to expose these opposing forces of metrical parallelism. Often enough in the opening March of *The Soldier's Tale*, for example, the notated bar line shifts rapidly in order that repeated melodic fragments might be notated in a parallel fashion.

The "tick-tock of a neural metronome"

Disruptions of the meter in Stravinsky's music, triggered often enough by the sorts of metrical displacements traced in example 8.1a, b, c, and d, affect the listener *physically*. And this is because of *entrainment*, the psychological means by which meter is internalized. Entrainment speaks directly to the impact of Stravinsky's music on our senses, the excitement that is likely to be generated by the rhythmic and metrical processes discussed just above.

Meter and sound vibration penetrate mind and body, of course, doing so by way of the eardrum which, in response to these impulses, moves back and forth sympathetically. The impulses are converted into neural signals, traveling first to the brain stem and then to the brain. Expectations of the sort mentioned above (those of metrical parallelism) are raised, confirmed, or frustrated in the prefrontal cortex. Music *floods* the brain, quite literally, engaging all regions as well as all neural subsystems.

Crucially, however, it is not just that music echoes and is constrained by our physical selves, our biological clock mechanisms. More dramatic and consequential still is something like the reverse of this equation, namely, that our internal clocks echo and become synchronized with metrical pulsation. These clocks are oscillations or back-and-forth motions in the main, it being understood that on the other side of the equation, meter consists not of pulsation alone, but rather of at least two levels of pulsation, with the slower one marking off the faster one into equal spans of two or three beats. The result is the familiar strong-weak or down-up alternation. (Even with a series of ticks or taps that are phenomenally identical, listeners will tend to automatically "group" them in twos, threes, and fours. Such reflexive behavior, studied by psychologists for well over a century, has been termed "subjective rhymicization".)

Yet the seat of this remarkable capacity to internalize meter may be our brains rather than any biological timepiece. It may have to do with neural networks, as the music scholar Robert Gjerdingen has proposed, networks that oscillate as a matter of course.[4] In Gjerdingen's computer model set up in 1989, the ebb and flow of excitation and inhabitation between two neural populations is made to enter into an up-and-down oscillation, the "tick-tock of a neural metronome." If the rate of excitation and inhibitions between populations is doubled, the metronome will beat a three/four waltz time. Greater metrical complexities are achieved by adding additional neural populations.

How any of this might work in reality still remains something of a mystery. Yet it is evident that, in one way or another, we as listeners *entrain* to meter, which in turn becomes *physically* a part of us. Entrainment is automatic (reflexive) as well as subconscious (or preconscious). Like walking, running, dancing, and breathing, meter is a kind of motor behavior, as the theorist Justin London has described it. Once entrained, meter is abandoned by the listener only in the face of strong contradictory evidence. Hence, with special reference to Stravinsky's music and the displacements of the above fragment in example 8.1, the explosive potential of an actual disruption of a meter, the physical effect a disturbance of this kind can have on the listener. The physical character of much of Stravinsky's music arises accordingly, that is, from entrainment and from the challenges to or disturbances of an attuned metrical grid.

9. Performance Practice and Aesthetic Belief

Beginning in the 1920s and 30s, Stravinsky turned increasingly to the performance of his music. The difficulties he faced in doing so, whether at the podium or the piano, had mainly to do with the prevailing norms, standards of interpretation that were very different from his own. Chief among the difficulties was the maintenance of an even tempo and the avoidance of any fluctuation of the beat. "Tempo is the principle item," Stravinsky replied when asked about performance problems; "my music can survive just about anything but wrong or uncertain tempo".[1]

Early on the composer adopted what has become known as a *strict performing style*. He favored straight, unnuanced readings not only of his own music, but of the classics as well, the instrumental music of the 18th century. In this, he anticipated more general modernist trends in the 20th century, the preferences for a strict approach to all manner of repertory. Yet the requirements for a steady beat in the performance of much of his music were not therefore a fad, a reflection merely of the times. Nor are they traceable to what critics have alleged to have been an autocratic, "anti-humanistic" disposition. Rather, they serve musical ends. They can be traced to specifically musical phenomena.

Indeed, the rationale behind these requirements lies close to the surface. If, in Stravinsky's music, a juxtaposition of distinct blocks of material was to make itself felt, then the tempo had to be maintained strictly from one repetition to the next. And if, by the same token, the metrical displacement of a theme or motive was to have its effect, then here, too, the tempo had to be maintained at an even pace. The point of the displacement would be lost if subjected to any "expressive fluctuation of the beat," as the philosopher Theodor Adorno phrased it in his lengthy critique of Stravinsky and his music.[2] The standard rubato could not be tolerated in this regard, adjustments capable of weakening the listener's sense of meter and alignment.

Rubato and nuance

And so the implications of Stravinsky's rhythmic innovations were felt most keenly in the area of expressive affect or rubato. Given the need for a strictly maintained beat, little allowance could be made for the conventions of expressive timing, the means by which, traditionally, performers have made their mediating presence felt. Consisting of small-scale cadential retardations and the like, these conventions may always have been part of music-making. Setting the issue on fire here, however, was the question of their motivation. To deviate from the regular was to be affected. It was to demonstrate engagement on the performer's part, the human capacity for arousal.

According to the psychologist Carl Seashore, the terms were among the most intimate known to music:

> In music and speech, pure tone, true pitch, exact intonation, perfect harmony, rigid rhythm, even touch, and precise time play a relatively small role. They are mainly points of orientation for art and nature. The unlimited resources for vocal and instrumental art lie in artistic deviation from the pure ... and the precise. This deviation from the exact is, on the whole, the medium for the creation of the beautiful—for the conveying of emotion.[3]

As a result, the nerve touched by these Stravinsky-inspired prohibitions against rubato and nuance was a sensitive one. The conflicts to which they led in matters of interpretation could not have had a more serious effect on the critical reaction to his music.

And the issue was by no means one of musical affect alone. Slight modifications of timing and punctuation, whether notated or coming by way of the performer alone, had served as a means of structure. Intensifying, often by exaggeration, the delays and accelerations already a part of the music (the delay of the note of suspension and its resolution in tonal music, for example), these rallentandos, ritardandos, ritenutos, and morendos had been expressions of structural clarification as well as engagement. They had served to clarify the boundaries of phrases and other large groupings. And it was generally understood that a performer intervened with a purpose of this kind as key. Modifications were not isolated effects (mere caprice or display on the performer's part), but a means toward a larger end. And artistic performances were weighed in this light—that is, by the extent to which they were "true" to the music, placed at the service of a convincing sense of structure.

The ideal could not have been more widely or firmly held. In the interests of a phrase and its articulation, the downbeat marking the end of a cadence might be delayed and then lengthened somewhat. This might occur minutely and almost imperceptibly as part of a hierarchy of such delays and lengthenings, with the weightiest coinciding with the larger phrases or sections. Not just structure plain and simple, but something of the psychology embedded within would be acknowledged and clarified as well. The overall impression gained of a performance could be that of a dramatic enactment, of performers acting out the events and processes internal to the music (cadences, resolutions, and the like). Performers themselves could be ensured a more active role in the process, with a sense of the human or personal enhanced.

Reading at sight, performers begin by parsing the music, drawing a mental image of its structure, and reacting expressively to that image. Unconscious and spontaneous rather than learned, memorized, and then applied in subsequent readings, the process comes "naturally" to the performer, and to a far greater extent than the deadpan or expressionless alternative. In fact, singing or playing totally without expression is exceedingly difficult, and performers asked to do this have invariably been observed to give way at some point to the familiar departures. Even Stravinsky, committed as he was to the virtues of playing in strict tempo, felt obliged to acknowledge (and accept) the irrepressible nature of expression, the residue that would have to remain even under the strictest of conditions.

Crucially, however, when applied to Stravinsky's music, the standard modifications of performance practice weakened structure. They obscured the juxtapositions, stratifications, and metrical alignments of Stravinsky's repeated themes, motives, and chords. And they were set aside quite deliberately by the composer for these very reasons. At odds with the core of his music, they were dismissed as a form of liberty. They were identified as a form of display, a sacrifice made for the sake of a performer's "feelings."

For the composer himself, the personal in music could not have taken on a worse set of connotations. What for the performer had been a matter of structure as well as engagement, had become one of engagement alone—indeed, one of self-indulgence. Conductors were always the most heavily censored in Stravinsky's many published remarks on the subject of interpretation. Unable to adapt themselves to a work, too many conductors "adapted the work to themselves … to their style, their mannerisms." Stravinsky tended to maintain that, in a performance of his own music, conductors had merely to sustain the beat evenly, watch for cues, and acknowledge the metrical irregularity, and the stress and phrase markings in as clean, crisp, and percussive a fashion as possible; anything else would blunt critical intent. What was required of the meter in a performance of Stravinsky's repeated and displaced themes, motives, and chords was mechanical precision. Fidelity was required, coolness with a sense of restraint. Notes were not to be slurred or tied into. In matters of articulation, a crisp, clean, and *secco* approach was essential if the bite of the invention was to be given its due.

Tempo was a factor as well. The larger tempo changes marking the individual tableaux and sections of *The Wedding* often involved the simplest proportions in order that they, too, might imply the tightest of controls. The simplicity of these ratios guaranteed such an effect. And this was especially true of the 1918-19 penultimate version of *The Wedding* for two cimbaloms, pianola, and percussion. Here, the mechanical piano could provide both the meter and the changes in tempo with an interpretation that was razor-sharp in its accuracy. Stravinsky's many transcriptions for the player piano date from the 1920s, as do the many contracts he negotiated with manufacturers of perforated piano rolls. (A chronology of these negotiations with the Pleyel and Aeolian Companies could fill a hefty volume.) However lucrative these contracts from a financial standpoint, their motivation was primarily aesthetic. As Stravinsky later explained in his *Autobiography*, he had been "anxious to find a means of imposing some restriction on the notorious liberty" that had been widespread in performances at the time. His preoccupation with the pianola (later, the pleyela with the Pleyel company) was less with the idiom itself than with its ability to transmit with pinpoint precision. Given the demand of his music for such precision, why should he continue to persevere with performers and the traditions of a performance practice? What need was there for an *interpretation* of his music?

Stravinsky's lifelong battle with rubato and nuance begins here, in fact, not with the aesthetics, necessarily, but rather with these practical matters of performance. Lamenting the "deforming" effects of nuance, he drew a sharp distinction between "execution" and "interpretation," citing the latter as "the root of all the errors, all the sins, all the misunderstandings that interpose themselves between the musical work and the listener."[4] Still later, in his *Conversations with Stravinsky* (1959), he softened his stance somewhat, acknowledging the existence of a "Romantic tradition" that stood in opposition to a "Classic tradition." While the former depended "strongly on mood and interpretation," the latter, which included the performing requirements of his own works, was closely tied to the dance. Our point here is that it is only in conjunction with concrete musical concerns of this kind that something of the relentless nature of his pursuit of a strict performing practice can be appreciated.

No doubt, Stravinsky's music offers less opportunity for expressive variation than the music of many of his predecessors and contemporaries. To a degree far greater than with the music of the 19th and early 20th centuries, the performers of his music are "executants" or "transmitters" rather than "interpreters" (the role of the solo violin in the Royal March of *The Soldier's Tale* can come vividly to mind in this connection). And this may explain in part the relative infrequency of performances of the Piano Concerto (1924), the *Capriccio* (1928), and the Violin Concerto (1931). At the same time, however, an expressive response to the relevant structural characteristics of his music need be no less effective than a response to the characteristics, say, of Chopin's Nocturnes. A fairly straight reading of *The Soldier's Tale* can be as expressive as a strongly nuanced one of Chopin's Nocturne in E-flat. What counts in any given instance is less the amount of rubato or nuance than its appropriateness. Essential is that an interpretation be felt as arising out of the circumstances of the music, as shaping and making sense of those conditions.

Indeed, to an extent no less than with Stravinsky's insistence on a strict performance approach, the composer's aesthetic convictions are rooted in the concrete detail and making of his own music. His forays into matters of aesthetics were provoked accordingly—that is, by the reactions of conductors, performers, and critics during the 1910s, 20s, and 30s. In the face of much hostile criticism about the lack of expression in his music, he wished to proclaim the meaning and significance of his music all the same. And he did so notwithstanding the "cold and heartless" means by which, necessarily in his music, meaning and significance were conveyed.

Music was very much "a world unto itself" for Stravinsky. His notorious dictum about the powerlessness of music "to express anything at all" was later amended to read "music expresses itself." Meaning and significance were not denied, only attempts to come to terms verbally with the underlying connection of music. Sensed and felt, that connection was given immediately in experience; Stravinsky's scattered reflections on the matter of music's deeper meaning point to an aesthetics of the "specifically musical." Music's expressive qualities were qualities at all "only in musically expressive form," only as they are expressed in music.

Distrustful of attempts at translation, of the life such attempts could assume on their own, Stravinsky feared music's trivialization, its "debasement," abuse, and exploitation. Music itself was a creation, not just—or even primarily—a mirroring of something else:

> Composition is something entirely new *beyond* what can be called the composer's feelings ... does not [Ernst Cassirer] say somewhere that art is not an imitation, but a discovery, of reality? My objection to music criticism is that it usually directs itself to what it supposes to be the nature of the imitation—when it should be teaching us to learn and to love a new reality. A new piece of music *is* a new reality.[5]

The claim of a "new reality" on behalf of art or the musical work would seem to imply the idea of a transcendence. Music can be listened to and appreciated for its own sake ("just for the hell of it," as the literary theorist Terry Eagleton has expressed it), not for the uses to which it could be put, or the causes it could be made to serve. It is magically "free of the vulgar taint of utility".[6]

We should note, finally, that the "cold and heartless" features attending the performance of Stravinsky's music are not solely a matter of the beat and its strict observance. In concrete terms, features of this kind can be found everywhere, from the composer's instrumental choices (the omission of strings in *The Wedding* and the *Symphonies of Wind Instruments*, for example), to the use of the piano as an instrument of punctuation and percussion. In applications of various types of stratification, for example, brass and woodwind instruments, with their hardness of attack and variety of timbre, could better articulate the contrasts between the conflicting, superimposed layers. In *The Rite of Spring* traditional balances were upset altogether by these imperatives; brass and woodwind sections occupied the leading roles, while the string section occupied the accompanying ones. Stravinsky acknowledged these preferences even at the time of the conception of *The Rite of Spring*: strings were "too symbolic and representative of the human voice," he averred, while wind instruments, with their "drier tone," were "more precise and less endowed with facile expression." In the final 1923 version of *The Wedding* he conceded quite bluntly that he had not wanted "anything so human as strings." What he had sought was a complement to the "intransigent quality" of the material, a sharp, "percussive" approach in the instrumentation. In turn, the material and its instrumentation were designed as a complement to the unbending and archaic severity of the wedding rituals themselves.

10. Neoclassicism Born

My instinct is to recompose, and not only student's works, but also old masters' as well. When composers show me their music for criticism, all I can say is that I would have written it quite differently. Whatever interests me, whatever I love, I wish to make my own (I am probably describing a rare form of kleptomania). [Igor Stravinsky and Robert Craft, *Memories and Commentaries*.]

The suggestion that was to lead to *Pulcinella* (1920) came from Diaghilev one spring afternoon while we were walking together in the Place de la Concorde: "I have an idea that I think will amuse you ... I want you to look at some delightful eighteenth-century music with the idea of orchestrating it for a ballet." When he told me that the composer was Pergolesi [1710-36], I thought he must be deranged. I did promise to look, however, and to give him my opinion.

I looked, and I fell in love. My ultimate selection of pieces derived only partly from Diaghilev's examples, however, and partly from published editions, but I played through the whole of the available Pergolesi before making my choices.... I began without preconceptions or aesthetic attitudes, and I could not have predicted anything about the result. I knew that I could not produce a "forgery" of Pergolesi because my motor habits are so different; at best, I could repeat him in my own accent.

Pulcinella was my discovery of the past, the epiphany through which the whole of my late [neoclassical] work became possible. It was a backward look, of course—the first of many love affairs in that direction—but it was a look in the mirror, too. [Igor Stravinsky and Robert Craft, *Expositions and Developments*.]

So there *is* a dividing line, then, something–somethings–tangible distinguishing Stravinsky's neoclassicism from his Russian-period works. He tired of Russian folk versification. Or perhaps he tired of those reiterating Dorian tetrachords and their octatonic or diatonic/modal implications. Or else, as he said, he "fell in love," determined to seek an accommodation with the practices and conventions of certain hitherto neglected musical traditions. (We are prone to forget that Stravinsky's neoclassical "love affairs" with the music of the 18th-century Italian composer Giovanni Battista Pergolesi, Bach, Mozart, and Beethoven, among many others, were directed not so much at the material at hand, as at the always sought-after *accommodation*, at reinterpretation and *recomposition*. The object of his affection lay not so much with the music of the above-noted composers, as with appropriation, the "making his own" (his "rare form of kleptomania"). It lay less with his models than with his recomposition, his "accent"; and then less with his own music than with the *composing* of his own music.)

Unprecedented from a historical perspective, however, is the *non-immediacy* of these transient "love affairs," the *distance* that now separates Stravinsky from his models. (Compare, in this respect, the influence of his immediate predecessor Rimsky-Korsakov in *The Firebird* and even *Petrushka*; or Arnold Schoenberg's historically more natural preoccupation with his immediate past in the music of Mahler.) It is this non-immediacy which gives Stravinsky's neoclassicism its most distinctive, yet unexpected twist. Notwithstanding these studied encounters with the remote past, the impression gained of him is that of a loner, of a composer severed and set apart. Stravinsky would become as obsessively preoccupied with his newly found, uniquely fashioned forms of accommodation with Baroque and Classical music, as he was earlier with his "fabrication" of Russian folk-like material. In other words, notwithstanding these many and varied "love affairs"; the extraordinary *reach* in historical scope; the numerous and lengthy concert tours undertaken as a conductor and pianist (principally of his own music); the truly international, worldly air Stravinsky assumes as a result of all this traffic; despite these many circumstances, the impression gained of him is one of personal and artistic isolation.

Stravinsky remained aloof, strangely unaffected by the music of his contemporaries and immediate predecessors. Apart from some early borrowings from Debussy, the only truly contemporary piece of music which seems to have left an impression was Schoenberg's *Pierrot lunaire* (1912), a work for chamber ensemble and *Sprechstimme*, a milestone in German expressionism. He heard *Pierrot* while on a visit to Berlin with Diaghilev in December 1912, at which time he also met Schoenberg.

Indeed, so impressed was Stravinsky with Schoenberg's *Pierrot lunaire* that, on returning to France, he relayed his enthusiasm to Debussy and Maurice Ravel, and set about composing the *Three Japanese Lyrics* (1913). But Schoenberg's influence by way of *Pierrot* was to prove not only superficial (*Pierrot* was understood "instrumentally" or in an "impressionistic fashion," as Pierre Boulez later remarked), but also short-lived. For while Stravinsky later insisted that *Pierrot* had constituted "the great event of my life" and that he was aware of its being "the most prescient confrontation in my life," there is no evidence of a follow-through (after *Lyrics*). Indeed, incredible as it may now seem, not until after Schoenberg's death in 1951 did Stravinsky make any studied attempt to rekindle his early enthusiasm and familiarize himself with the music of Schoenberg and his two disciples, Anton Webern and Alban Berg.

For whatever the reasons, then, personal or professional, conscious or unconscious, this neoclassical impression of Stravinsky as a loner and its curious irony in light of all the many and varied "love affairs," "backward looks," or "raids on the past" remains indelible. Stravinsky was a tough, determined, defiant, and guarded composer (immensely guarded, as Robert Craft has commented, perhaps precisely because so "radically susceptible to personal influence").

Stravinsky's "love affairs"

Turning more specifically toward the musical implications of Stravinsky's neoclassicism, and his "love affairs" with the music of the 18th and early 19th centuries, we can make some general observations:

1. A new interest in instrumental invention divorced from the theater or from extra-musical implications. Stravinsky's attraction to the ballet continues, however, initially with *Pulcinella* and then *Apollo Musagetes* (1928). These ballets would be complemented by some hybrid theater works, most notably the opera/oratorio *Oedipus Rex* (1927), and the "melodrama" *Persephone* (1934).
2. A preoccupation with the tonal forms of the Baroque and Classical eras, with accommodations with sonata form, variation form, and fugue or fugato.
3. A breakdown of the rigid block structures of Russia-period works; or, more generally, a tendency to become less abrupt or "heterogeneous" in an effort to accommodate the Baroque and Classical forms alluded to just above. In addition, there are far fewer stratifications or polyrhythmic textures. When the latter do appear, they do so with fewer layers of fragments and chords repeating according to varying periods or spans. There is less conflict or irregularity.
4. A preoccupation with Baroque and Classical "surface gesture": typically Baroque patterns of toccata-like figuration or dotted rhythmic patterns; Classical formulations of "theme and accompaniment."
5. The demise of that earlier Russian-period preoccupation with the Dorian or minor tetrachord as melody. In octatonic or octatonic-diatonic settings, a preoccupation with triads and dominant-seventh chords (these latter often in novel guises, to be sure). Later neoclassical works exhibit various kinds of

major-minor ambiguity, often coming in the form of a clash between the major and minor thirds of a "tonic" triad.
6. A diatonic articulation which, while at times implicating the Phrygian and Aeolian modes, now rather persistently implies the major and minor scales of tonality.
7. An occasional yielding, in however parenthetical a fashion, to certain tonally functional relations, most notably, the dominant-tonic relation.

Pulcinella

The origins of *Pulcinella* can be traced to the Royal Public Library in Naples, Italy; more specifically, to a visit there in 1916 (or possibly 1917) by Leonid Massine, the dancer, choreographer, and associate of Diaghilev's. Massine intended to study the characters and plots of the Commedia dell' arte of 18th-century Italy. As the plan of action developed for a new ballet, he chose a comic episode featuring Pulcinella, the traditional hero of the Commedia. Following a series of intrigues involving love, deception, and disguise, Pulcinella marries Pimpenella.

As the musical complement to the new scenario, Diaghilev picked out 15 "unpublished instrumental works" (mostly string trios, canzones, and the like) on a subsequent visit to the Naples Conservatory. Although all these works were originally thought to have been composed by Pergolesi, this has since been disproven. Of the 21 selections that were ultimately to shape Stravinsky's *Pulcinella*, only 10 now appear to have been composed by Pergolesi. Of the remaining 11, some were composed by his contemporaries (or near-contemporaries), while others remain anonymous to this day.

On the eve of Stravinsky's trip to Paris in early May of 1919, Diaghilev cabled his colleague: "We have urgent business to discuss." The two had been quarreling about money and contracts, which was hardly new, even if the tone of their disagreements had grown increasingly harsh. No less characteristically, however, when they did finally meet in Paris, they did so with open arms. Three years had passed since the composer was last in the French capital, yet he would be staying only a fortnight. The time would be sufficient for him to familiarize himself with Diaghilev's 18th-century texts, to fall in love with them, and then to return to Morges.

Neoclassicism of a sort was born that moment in early May of 1919—the composer's recognition of the promise *Pulcinella* held for the future. Born, too, was the divide that would henceforth separate so many composers of the past century. There were those who, like Stravinsky, would seek an accommodation with the tonal tradition of the 18th and 19th centuries, and there were others who, on the other side of this divide, would follow Schoenberg's lead in dismantling and replacing tonality with "atonality" and various methods of serial composition.

In "atonal" and especially 12-tone music, pitches were imagined as having been "emancipated" from the "shackles of tonality" (to follow Schoenberg's favorite metaphor of tonal bondage), while diatonicism was replaced by the "total chromatic." At least in principle, each pitch gained "equality" in relation to the others, democratically or socialistically, as it were. Forfeited by such means, however, was the musical grammar and syntax that, for centuries, had been shared and inherited unconsciously from one generation of composers and listeners to the next. On the "progressive" side of this divide, the claim was that tonality had exhausted itself and had lost its ability to bear fruit. Schoenberg's Second Viennese School had emerged as a natural and logical consequence of the crisis.

A rivalry soon broke out between the two opposing sides (or warring factions), as the followers of Stravinsky and those of Schoenberg (and sometimes the principals themselves) began sparring in the popular press. In interviews conducted on his first American tour in January and February of 1925, Stravinsky, in veiled reference to Schoenberg's 12-tone system, complained of "modernists" who "worked with formulas instead of ideas."[1] His statements and others like it were often translated and circulated in the European press. Schoenberg responded several years later in a Foreword to his *Three Satires* (1928), addressing Stravinsky as *Der Kleine Modernsky* (Stravinsky was indeed small in stature, as was Schoenberg himself), and warning that the road to Rome could never be won by the "half measures" of "folklorists" and "quasi-tonalists."

In truth, neither Stravinsky nor Schoenberg had heard much of the other's music. They kept abreast of the critical commentary in journals and magazines, and weighted in accordingly. Undoubtedly, Stravinsky's remarks were often tongue-and-cheek, designed to keep his readership off balance. Crammed into hotel rooms, groups of journalists fired off questions eliciting responses in an atmosphere that was often carnival-like. The reporters egged him on–which is not to imply that Stravinsky's comments were not reflective of a reality, but only that they were partial, pieces of a much larger puzzle.

What Diaghilev wanted from Stravinsky's *Pulcinella* was a "stylish orchestration," nothing more or less. This was hardly Stravinsky's idea, however. He would be orchestrating Diaghilev's 18th-century texts, to be sure, and then adding some of his own choices from a variety of published sources. But he would also be *recomposing* "in my own accent." Ostinatos would be added here and there, along with rhythmic effects, and slight repetitions. In the opening Overture (as originally composed by Pergolesi), tonic and dominant pitches would be sustained at cadences. Blurring the distinction between these two functions, the sustained notes flattened out the harmony and allowed the rhythmic-metric scheme to come to the fore. Stravinsky entered some of these changes on the manuscript copies, as if he had been correcting a draft of his own music. Above all, he would be making a convincing whole out of what was initially a collection of individual pieces.

Nearly the entire *Pulcinella* was composed at the Maison Bornand in Morges, the birthplace of much of Stravinsky's late Russian-period music, including *Renard*, *Ragtime for Eleven Instruments*, *The Soldier's Tale*, and various versions of *The Wedding*. Squeezed into a small attic studio were the very instruments Ramuz had encountered earlier when working on the French translation of Stravinsky's Russian folk verses. *Pulcinella* was "the swan song of my Swiss years," as Stravinsky remembered it later, and so it undoubtedly was. It would be followed by the *Symphonies of Wind Instruments* (1920), a work still very much within the confines of the Russian period. Yet the spark of a new direction had been ignited, and there would be no pulling back. Having begun with Russian verses and a "fabrication" of Russian folk music, the years in Switzerland would end with neoclassicism.

The score of *Pulcinella* was completed on April 24, 1920; Stravinsky left for Paris on May 7 to help with the rehearsals. The first performance, on May 15 at the Paris Opera, was a considerable success. The costumes and sets, designed by Pablo Picasso, featured a moonlit, Cubist Naples, and drew universal praise as "one of the most beautiful stage settings ever made," to quote from Richard Buckle's *Diaghilev*. Massine danced the title role, Tamara Karsavina was Pimpinella, and Ansermet conducted an orchestra that had been reduced to 33 members. Clarinets and various forms of duplication had been omitted by the composer to approximate the more intimate sound and volume of an 18th-century ensemble.

The reviews of Stravinsky's music were mixed. Some critics attacked the composer as a *pasticheur* (an artist who imitates the style of another), while others chided him for betraying "modernism" and "his true Russian heritage." Yet there were many who praised his audacity. The conservative critic, Reynaldo Hahn, described *Pulcinella* as "a graceful, strange, and seductive paraphrase." "I hasten to add," he wrote, "that Monsieur Stravinsky has never given proof of greater talent than in *Pulcinella*."[2] In the ears and eyes of the public, Stravinsky had regained center stage in the world of contemporary art music.

11. Neoclassicism (I); Early Years

Destined for Carantec, a beach town in Brittany, France, Stravinsky and his family set out from the Maison Bornand in Morges for the last time on the morning of June 8, 1920. There were now four children. Milène, a second daughter, had been born on January 15, 1914. Soon after Katya had given birth to Milène, however, she was rushed to a sanatorium with tuberculosis in her right lung, the disease that had plagued her as a child. She recovered reasonably enough after a three-month stay, but her prognosis remained a source of worry.

In Paris toward the end of July, Stravinsky, Katya, and Katya's sister had come up empty-handed in their quest for suitable and permanent housing. This was before meeting up with the fashion designer Gabrielle "Coco" Chanel, a recent acquaintance of the composer's. On a temporary basis, Chanel offered them Bel Respiro, her villa outside Paris in Garches. An offer too generous to refuse under the circumstances, it was gratefully accepted, and the Stravinsky family moved into their new accommodations sometime in September. Awkwardly, however, an affair ensued soon thereafter between Stravinsky and Coco, launched presumably out of her apartment at the Ritz Hotel in central Paris.

This was not all. Still more consequential in these matters of intimacy was the affair struck up later that year with Vera Sudeykina, *nee* de Bosset, a Russian immigrant and acquaintance of Diaghilev's. De Bosset would become Stravinsky's mistress for the next 17 or so years, joining him on innumerable concert tours, until finally marrying him in 1940 in Boston, of all places, where the composer had traveled the previous year to deliver the Charles Eliot Norton lectures at Harvard. His departure from Europe in September of 1939 had less to do with the declarations of war there, than with an excruciating series of personal tragedies that had befallen him in 1938-39. His first daughter, Mika, had died of tuberculosis in November of 1938. Katya, by then crippled from this family curse, succumbed to it only months later, on March 3, 1939. And the death of the composer's aged mother, Anna Kirillovna, followed on June 7, 1939. "I survived only by composing," Stravinsky responded when asked about this series of calamities.[1] He would later claim that his ability to compose during this period furnished proof of the validity of his aesthetic convictions about the self-sufficiency of music, music's ability to stand alone as a "world unto itself."

Religious re-awakening

Back in Paris at the dawn of the new year (1921), Stravinsky was again losing hope of finding suitable quarters for his family. His luck turned in February, however, when the Pleyel Piano Company offered him the attic of their office-factory in the rue Rochechouart as a studio. His cimbalom and percussion instruments were duly installed, and he was soon at work again on the third version of *The Wedding*, the mechanized one for pianola, harmonium, two cimbaloms, and percussion. But he was growing dissatisfied with this version as well, even though an instrumental draft had been completed of the first two tableaux. On a brighter note, he was able to sign a six-year contract with the Pleyel Company to transcribe his complete works for the mechanical pleyela (the Pleyel Company's version of the player piano). The contract was worth 3000 francs a month, a handsome sum at the time.

The Stravinsky family moved again in May, this time to the Basque town of Anglet at the southwestern tip of France. From there they moved to nearby Biarritz, and from there, in 1924, to an upscale address in Nice, the Villa des Roses in the Boulevard Carnot. ("At what a price," Stravinsky winced in a letter to Ramuz; "I do not even dare to type it.") The Anglet-Biarritz area harbored a Russian immigrant community and a large Russian Orthodox Church, surroundings that may have been of some significance to Katya at the time. It was here, too, that the composer, himself in need of a measure of stability and calm in his life, began his prayerful return to Orthodoxy. (He had left the Church in 1910.) As with many Russian exiles, the Church offered a way of maintaining contact with the Russia that had all but disappeared with the Bolshevik coup of 1917. Stravinsky's infidelities may also have played a role in this return, as Robert Craft has suggested. A guilty conscience and a desire to seek redemption may have forced his hand.

Especially in Nice, where the collection of icons and other religious relics reached its peak (as many as 50 such artifacts were assembled, according to Stravinsky's biographer Stephen Walsh), the mood grew increasingly devout and sacramental. Stravinsky became a communicant of the Orthodox Church in 1926 while playing host to an Orthodox priest at the Villa des Roses. For nearly five years, Father Nikolai Podosenov took up residence in a separate apartment there, doing so very nearly as a member of the Stravinsky household.

Hand in hand with these new devotions came a new, humbled attitude toward art as "honest labor," musical composition as a craft pursued dutifully in the ears and eyes of God—A la gloire de DIEU, as this sentiment is expressed on the dedication page of his *Symphony of Psalms* (1930). Order and authority were now important to the composer, "the medieval idea of the artist as a humble, anonymous artisan erecting his cathedrals to the greater glory of God," to quote from Walsh's biography.[2] Some of this may have come by way of Jacques Maritain's *Art et scolastique* (1920), which Stravinsky may have read at the time of its publication. In it, Maritain sought to resurrect the Thomist tradition of the Roman Church, casting the thoughts of various Medieval scholiasts in a modern light. A Catholic convert from Protestantism, Maritain lectured in philosophy at the Institut Catholique in Paris.

In turn, these new artistic sensibilities were linked to the aesthetic beliefs discussed briefly in Chapter 9. Formalist in the main, these beliefs, long held by the composer, had begun to crystallize in a form that he now wished to proclaim aloud. Behind the desire to publicize these matters of philosophy were his anxieties about the expectations of audiences steeped in the operas and symphonic repertory of the later 19th century, the music of Wagner, Liszt, Brahms, and Mahler. It seemed essential that the stage be set for something less immediately personal or emotionally charged, music moored in the more remote past and conceived with different assumptions about performance, reception, and even the meaning of music. (In contrast to music as *representation*, formalists like Stravinsky held that the elements and passions of music were specific to it and its "forms." Music was "suprapersonal and superreal," as Stravinsky expressed it later in his *Expositions and Developments*; as such, it was something "beyond verbal meanings and verbal descriptions." Although more rigorously thought out than the art for art's sake philosophy that had prevailed at the time of *Mir iskusstva*, formalism can nonetheless be viewed as an extension of the latter.)

The first neoclassical declaration of these formalist principles came in "Some Ideas About My Octuor," a mini-manifesto first published (oddly enough) in English in an American journal, *The Arts*. Referring to his *Octet* (1923) as "a musical object," the composer dismissed "literary" and "picturesque" ramifications altogether, and insisted that "this sort of music has no other aim than to be sufficient in itself." The tone, stiff and hardened (even puritanical), softened somewhat in his next outing, a short lecture prefacing his performances (with his son Soulima) of the Concerto for Two Solo Pianos. These readings began with the premiere of the Concerto on November 21, 1935, in Paris. To demand from the Concerto, Stravinsky asserted,

> emotions of a general kind—joy, sorrow, sadness, something to dream about—would be to deprecate music by assigning it a comparably utilitarian purpose. Why not love it for itself

alone? Music needs no assistance. It is self-sufficient. Don't look for anything in it beyond what it contains.[3]

And Stravinsky would insist on the relevance of these aesthetic ideals to his earlier Russian-period works. In the case of *The Wedding*, a great many descriptive factors can come to mind: grace notes that imitate a gasp or sob, octatonic scale patterns that, coloring the diatonic, mimic the sound of a peasant band. Often enough, too, the repetition in *The Wedding* can seem unrelenting, to project an air of rigidity, stasis, and intractability. Beyond these metaphorical descriptions and analogies, however, the expressive qualities of *The Wedding* and of Stravinsky's music generally, as well as the ability of these qualities to stir emotionally (passionately), are matters not readily open to verbal translation. We are moved synthetically and essentially by what a piece of music is, Stravinsky insisted, not by what it could or might possibly *represent*. And the aesthetic rapture that can take hold can do so regardless of a piece's character, be it one of sadness, joy, exhilaration, longing, or intractability. Whatever the character, the source of our delight lies elsewhere.

The expressive qualities associated with Stravinsky's music are not something external to the music–in other words, impulses which, lying to the outside, obtain a form of portrayal within. They are inherent. They defy scrutiny not because they are too definite or too indefinite for words, but because their definiteness is entirely musical. They are feelings at all only by virtue of their expression in music.

Much of this is part and parcel of a formalist approach, as we have suggested, an aesthetics of the "specifically musical," as Eduard Hanslick characterized it in *The Beautiful in Music* (1854), and the sort of understanding to which Stravinsky himself would subscribe with stubborn insistence for the remainder of the century.

Stravinsky's neoclassicism was *non-immediate*, as we have observed. It bypassed the late Romantics (Brahms, Wagner, Mahler) and went directly to Bach and the Classical style of the late 18th and early 19th centuries. This was its bread and butter. Stravinsky borrowed from the forms of these categories: fugue, sonata, theme-and-variations, and so forth. And he borrowed from the language of tonality as well, with its major and minor scales. Always, however, an element of restraint prevailed. He distrusted and felt ill at ease with the emotional turmoil of the Romantics, their heaviness of mind, spirit, and means. (During the 1920s he developed the habit of mispronouncing Mahler as "Malheur," which means "misfortune" in French.) He intended his music to honor God, not humankind. He looked outward in his music, not within. ("I am not mirror struck by my mental faculties," he once wrote; "my interest passes immediately to the object, the thing made.") What mattered was directness, clarity, and purity of expression. Simplicity mattered. Economy, concision, and forthrightness.

Schoenberg, his nemesis, grew to resent Stravinsky's highly publicized neoclassicism. He, too, adopted the forms of the Baroque and Classical eras. And he borrowed from the textures of the Classical style as well, the theme and its accompanying figures, its continuing or developing variation. But his musical language of atonality and serialism was entirely new, revolutionary. He believed himself to be the heir to the German stem that had begun with Bach: Haydn-Mozart-Beethoven-Brahms-Wagner-Mahler. He thought Stravinsky's neoclassicism flimsy and superficial, the products themselves, "half measures" devoid of substance or historical significance.

Octet for Wind Instruments

On a visit to Biarritz in 1922, Sergei Koussevitzky, compatriot and future conductor of the Boston Symphony Orchestra (starting in 1924), invited Stravinsky to compose and conduct something new for an upcoming concert series in Paris. Stravinsky had been at work on an "instrumental sonata," as he called it, which would eventually become the Octet for Wind Instruments (1923), and the piece which he would indeed be conducting at Koussevitzky's invitation on October 18, 1923, at the Paris Opera. The success he enjoyed with the Octet was considerable, far greater than either he or Koussevitzky had anticipated. To focus the sound of his music within the vast expanse of the Opera stage, a screen was placed directly behind the eight instrumentalists. The novelty of the experience must have been sensed by all. The modernist composer famous for his giant-size scores for the ballet theater was now at work composing and conducting these cozy little pieces with their obvious, surface-level references to Bach and the Classical style.

Not surprisingly, a good deal of confusion reigned at the time about the composer's creative whereabouts. The first performance of The Wedding had taken place several months prior to the Octet, while Renard was given its premiere a year earlier. Picking up the scent of an orientation must have been all but impossible even for those informed of the twists and turns of Stravinsky's earlier works.

In the Octet's first movement the composer's "appetite" was whetted by his "rediscovery" of sonata form, while, with the third and concluding movement, Bach's two-part inventions lay in the remote back of his mind: "The terseness and lucidity of the inventions were an ideal of mine at the time, and I sought to keep those qualities uppermost in my composition".[4]

Yet it is the Octet's second movement, Andante, that offers the clearest illustration of accommodation, of the mixing of Stravinsky's past (what it was that was gradually making Stravinsky sound like Stravinsky), with tonality and the Classical style; see example 11.1. The formal apparatus fits the Classical model of a theme and its variations, while the theme's presentation is a typical theme-and-accompaniment setting. Looking to the past as well as the future, however, the theme is *wholly octatonic*. At rehearsal no.25, its first phrase is transposed by a minor third, guaranteeing continued confinement to the given octatonic scale: in ascending order, A-Bb-C-C#-D#-E-F#-G-(A).

EXAMPLE 11.1: Octet, octatonic theme, D-minor accompaniment

Beneath the octatonic theme, however, the accompaniment implies D minor (or quasi-D minor). And the "tonic" pitch D along with the "tonic" triad (D F A) lie outside of the given octatonic scale. And so, the result is a kind of static clashing or *superimposition* of the octatonic theme over its quasi D-minor accompaniment. The theme's closing F# neatly unites the octatonic scale with the D-minor accompaniment by way of a *tierce de Picardie*.

There are many complications to this scheme, however. As the graph below the musical quotation reveals in example 11.1, there are pitches between the two scales that clash and others that are held in common. Paramount among the latter are the pitches of the triad (A

C♯ E). While the latter is outlined by the octatonic theme, it serves as the dominant in D minor.

Hence, neoclassicism imposes itself in the form of an interaction between the octatonic scale of the variation theme and the D-minor tonality. The two are brought together in the final measure by a "tonic resolution" on D, with the shared or intersecting F♯ delineating the *tierce de Picardie* inflection. Although F♯, the major third, is octatonic, it relates to the D-minor tonality by way of the *tierce*. Hence the peculiarity of Stravinsky's neoclassical dominant, not only here in the Andante, but in subsequent neoclassical contexts as well.

Stravinsky the pianist

Stravinsky's success with the *Octet* led Koussevitzky to inquire about the possibility of a repeat performance. Giving it some thought, Stravinsky settled on a concerto this time, specifically, the *Concerto for Piano and Wind Instruments* (1924). The decision was a fateful one, given Koussevitzky's suggestion that the composer appear as soloist rather than conductor:

> I hesitated at first, fearing I should not have enough time to perfect my technique as a pianist, and to acquire the endurance necessary to perform a work demanding sustained effort. But I am by nature rather tempted by anything needing prolonged effort, and prone to persist in overcoming difficulties; and as also the prospect of creating my work myself, and thus establishing the manner in which I wanted it to be played, greatly attracted me, I decided finally to accept the proposal.[5]

In addition to conducting, Stravinsky would now be practicing and performing at the piano. And he would be doing so, as it turned out, for the next 15 or so years. Which is not to imply that he was ever a virtuoso pianist, or that the conductors close to him (Ansermet and Monteux, for example) were not a good deal more skillful than he with the baton. But he needed the income, as he later explained; he would not be composing blockbuster scores for the Ballets Russes in the near future. And he relished the opportunity of presenting his music the way he thought it should be presented. Such an ambition lay behind the hundreds of hours he would also be expending on his perforated piano rolls in the rue Rochechouart. These latter, too, were a means of securing something like definitive performances, ones capable of capturing his ideals of a strictly held beat with a minimum of nuance. Quite apart from the financial compensation, in other words, it was the opportunity of fashioning a practice that attracted him.

For five years from the day of the Piano Concerto's first performance on May 22, 1924 (with Koussevitzky conducting), Stravinsky reserved the role of soloist exclusively for himself. On tour in the United States in early 1925, he performed the Concerto 25 times in cities on the East Coast and the Midwest, charging $1000 on each occasion. (Koussevitzky would conduct the American premiere in Boston, just as he had conducted the world premiere the preceding summer in Paris.) Later in 1925, Stravinsky's performances of the Concerto began to overlap with those of the *Piano Sonata* (1925). Among many other venues, he performed the *Sonata* at the Festival of the International Society of Contemporary Music (I.S.C.M.) held in Venice in 1925. Schoenberg was there as well, conducting his *Serenade* (1924), but Stravinsky failed to attend. Schoenberg did attend Stravinsky's performance of his *Sonata* on September 7, but walked out midway through, if we can trust the recollection of the British musicologist Edward Dent, who was serving as Chairman of the Society.

The *Sonata* was soon followed by the *Serenade en la*, also for piano, with its homage to Beethoven in the second movement. Still further along, the *Capriccio* for piano and orchestra (1929)–a friendlier piece than the Piano Concerto–followed the *Serenade en la*, while the Concerto for Two Solo Pianos (1935) followed the

Capriccio. Stravinsky's partner in performances of the Concerto was his son, Soulima, who by 1935 had been assisting his father in a range of tasks, including proofreading and playing through the accompanying parts of various works in progress. Like his father, Soulima was a formidable sight-reader at the piano.

Most reflective of what Stravinsky called his "back to Bach movement" were the first movements of his Piano Concerto, the *Piano Sonata*, and the "Dumbarton Oaks" *Concerto in E-flat* (much later in 1938). Entirely reminiscent of Bach in the Piano Concerto's first movement is the toccata-like figuration (neighbor-note figuration, more specifically) on the very first page of the piano solo, in the key of D major/minor and sustained over a stepwise motion in the "bass." But although Bach-like in appearance, the "bass line" is largely out of step harmonically with the figuration on top; it clashes with the latter and, indeed, can seem to be displaced relative to it. There are syncopated ragtime figures later in this movement, patterns which, repeated, conflict polyrhythmically with the spans of other reiterating fragments. And there are lengthy passages of chords being exchanged rapidly between left and right hands, which can bring to mind Bach's Piano Concerto in D minor.

But what seems to have excited and fascinated critics and audiences alike was the enormous energy the composer seemed to be expending while playing works such as the Piano Concerto's first movement. "Endurance" of a particular kind was required of this movement's fast, perpetual motion, the stamina to stay on track while fighting off the reflexive inclinations of nuance and expression, the temptation to interpret and "explain" (as discussed in chapter 9). Critics complained about the unnatural, machine-like quality of Stravinsky's playing. (A sense of this quality may yet be gained from recordings preserved from the 1930s.)[6] But the playing cannot be divorced from the music. To have performed the rhythmic intricacies of this first movement in anything but a strict tempo would have been to misinterpret them. The point of the rhythmic play would have been lost.

Other impressions of Stravinsky as a composer and conductor

during this period are no less insightful, especially in the United States where, at the time of his tour in 1925, he and his music were relatively unknown. Stravinsky was short in stature, as we have noted, yet trim and agile. Fond of fine apparel, he dressed fashionably during the 1920s and 30s. In conversation, he could seem preoccupied, sometimes with a rather severe, determined look. In *Down a Path of Wonder* (2006), Robert Craft recalled the composer as hypertense and edgy to the point of fretfulness, fearing the worst of any given situation.

To Lawrence Gilman, the music critic of the *New York Herald Tribune*, Stravinsky seemed "a slight, nervous, baldescent, goggled, and pleasantly homely figure." Quoted from Stephen Walsh's biography, the following appeared in the *Boston Post* in January of 1925:

> Not from any outward appearance might this be the man from whom has come such devastating music. There is in Mr. Stravinsky's aspect and manner, in his extraordinarily rapid, almost mechanical motions, in his slight body and his eyes that seemed just to have left off peering in a microscope, more to suggest the entomologist rather than the musician. That he is an intellect, an enormously developed mental machine, seems the most obvious conclusion.

And according to Olin Downes, the music critic of *The New York Times* (February 6, 1925), audiences were "stirred" above all by the rhythm of Stravinsky's Piano Concerto, and by "the magnificent virtuosity of Mr. Stravinsky's performance—he seemed to have endless speed, power, precision at command, and was himself a complete rival orchestra." Downes was less pleased with what he called the replacement of "emotion" by "ruthless, driving energy." He decried the "imperious and sardonic" features of the "modern temperament."

12. Neoclassicism (II): High Watermarks

The oddest chapter in Stravinsky's musical biography may well be the one that surrounds the opera/oratorio, *Oedipus Rex* (1927). The initial spark for this venture seems to have originated with Jean Cocteau's *Antigone*, a fairly strict reading and translation of the Sophocles play that was first staged in 1922. Intrigued by this effort, Stravinsky inquired about the possibility of undertaking a similar experiment with *Oedipus Rex*, one that would involve condensing and translating this second play into French. Long an enthusiast of the Ballets Russes, Cocteau jumped at the prospect of a collaboration along the lines outlined by the composer. (The two had been friends for a number of years.) But the task would be far from straightforward. Cocteau would oblige his friend, but it would take him three revised drafts to do so. What Stravinsky wanted was a very traditional script (hardly Cocteau's métier, as Stravinsky conceded at the time), something along the lines of a Handel libretto, with arias, recitatives, and choruses. (Years later with *The Rake's Progress*, 1948-51, in Los Angeles, the composer would be requiring much the same of his librettist, W. H. Auden, even if his models were a bit more specifically the Classical style and late 18th-century opera).

In 1926, however, Stravinsky would also be asking Jean Danielou, a Jesuit priest studying theology at the Sorbonne, to translate Cocteau's French into Latin. (The Latin would not be a translation of the original Greek, in other words.) Infused with universality and a certain monumental character, Latin embodied gravity, or "gravitas," to use the current term. For Catholics, Latin was the language of religious ritual. And for those members of his prospective audiences insufficiently familiar with either Latin or Sophocles' play (or both), Stravinsky would be providing them with short summaries of the action at critical points. These latter synopses would be delivered in the vernacular (French in France) by a narrator or Speaker, who would also be appearing in evening dress. Set apart from the drama in this way, the Speaker's role is an intriguing one, even if it tired easily, as seems to have been the case with Stravinsky. The composer grew to dislike Cocteau's prose as well, which he thought haughty and pretentious. But the Speaker's interventions are indispensable, given that the music is paced by them.

Monumentality was not the only feature drawing the composer to "Ciceronian Latin"—so named because it reflected Cicero's influence on the classical Latin language. Impersonal and unsullied by conventional sentiment, Latin was a kind of pure sound for the text-setting Stravinsky. Just as with the folk verses of his Russian-period works, he would be bypassing the meaning of the words and going directly to the sounds of the syllables. As before, these sounds would be activating his "musical saliva:"

> What a joy it is to compose music to a language of convention, almost of ritual, the very nature of which imposes a lofty dignity! One no longer feels dominated by the phrase, the literal meaning of the words. Cast in an immutable mold which adequately expresses their value, they do not require any further commentary. The texts thus becomes purely phonetic material for the composer. He can dissect it at will and concentrate all his attention on its primary constituent element—that is to say, on the syllable.[1]

The austerity of *Oedipus* as an opera was further enhanced by Stravinsky's stage directions, which left the actor/singers behind masks (as in Greek theater), moving only with their heads and arms, and addressing the audience in an icy "still-life" confrontation with fate. (Stravinsky's eldest son Theodore, already an aspiring artist and designer, was entrusted with the décor.) At the opening of *Oedipus*, a chorus alerts the King of the plague at Thebes. A prideful Oedipus assures the populace of his ability to uncover its cause. But a Messenger arrives to announce breathlessly that it is the King himself who has caused the catastrophe, sparking the anger of the Gods. Unbeknownst, the King has murdered his father and married his mother.

In the end, however, *Oedipus* was premiered not as an opera but in concert form as an oratorio. Its first performance on May 30, 1927, at the Théâtre Sarah Bernhardt in Paris, was preceded by a trial run in the grand salon of the Princess de Polignac; in place of the orchestra, Stravinsky accompanied the singers at the piano. Née Winnaretta Singer, heiress to the Singer sewing machine fortune in the United States, the Princess had become Stravinsky's most loyal and generous patron during the 1920s, offering her salon on numerous occasions for auditions. It was she who, during the difficult years of World War I, had commissioned *Renard*.

Which brings us to the strangest part yet of this episode. Danceless and devoid of movement, Stravinsky's oratorio would be produced by Diaghilev and the Ballets Russes on a double bill that included a newly designed *Firebird*. That such a contradiction could have been scheduled at the time seems scarcely conceivable. Not surprisingly, the audience—a dance audience on both occasions, at the avant-premiere and the premiere—reacted coolly to the new work, undoubtedly more out of bewilderment than anything else.

But the problem was that, from the start, Stravinsky had intended *Oedipus* to serve as an anniversary gift to the impresario on the occasion of his 20th year in the theater. He had sought to keep the undertaking secret for as long as possible, primarily as a means of avoiding the usual conflicts and rows. When Diaghilev learned of the project, he was not amused. "Un cadeau très macabre", was his response; a very morbid gift.

Disagreements between Diaghilev and Stravinsky continued into the following season of the Ballets Russes. The composer's new ballet, *Apollo Musagetes* (1928), was commissioned by an American patron, Elizabeth Sprague Coolidge, and was first performed on April 27 at the Library of Congress in Washington, D.C. The performance by the Ballets Russes followed later that year in June. Needless to say, this was not the sort of arrangement to which

Diaghilev had been accustomed. And he reacted as he had earlier with *The Wedding* and *Renard*, theater projects that had likewise been conceived outside of himself and the Ballets Russes. He regarded such occasions as acts of disloyalty and ingratitude. A snippet of conversation on the matter of *Apollo*'s commission survives from this period:

> Diaghilev: Cette americaine [Elizabeth Sprague Coolidge] est sourde. (This American [Elizabeth Sprague Coolidge] is totally deaf.)
> Stravinsky: Elle est sourde, mais elle pais. (She is deaf but she pays.)
> Diaghilev: Tu pense toujours de l'argent. (You always think of money.)

Ultimately, however, it would be *Apollo*'s performance in Paris that both Diaghilev and the composer would regard as its true premiere. Featured in the title role was Sergei Lifar, while the choreographer was George Balanchine, the "ballet master" who would be designing Stravinsky's ballets for the next 30 or so years.

One of Stravinsky's later recollections of Diaghilev was that of an intensely sensual individual. Petty and childish at times, Diaghilev's resentments had long been a source of exasperation for Stravinsky and the many others who worked with him on a regular basis. Chronically suspicious of the motives of his associates, Diaghilev was forever fearful of being sidelined and "betrayed." Quick to take offense and bear a grudge (as was Stravinsky, often enough), Diaghilev was always very much in touch with, as well as trusting of, his raw, immediate senses and impressions. By 1929, he and the composer were no longer on speaking terms.

The impresario died unexpectedly on August 19, 1929, of diabetes, a disease that had apparently gone undiagnosed. He passed away in a hotel room in Venice ("like a vagabond," as Ansermet expressed it at the time), and was subsequently laid to rest there on the island cemetery of San Michele Stravinsky and his family mourned his death, doubtless in memory of what he had meant and all that he had made possible. Few had gauged as adroitly the depth of Stravinsky's genius. And Diaghilev had done so at the very start, with Stravinsky's *Scherzo fantastique* and the two orchestrations for Fokine's *Les Sylphides*. Not long before his death, Diaghilev continued to update himself on the nature of Stravinsky's art:

> Stravinsky is the living embodiment of a true enthusiasm for, a true love of art; the personification of eternal striving .... he is constantly on the move, seeking out at every step how to deny the very thing that he has been in his previous work.[2]

Eclectic pieces of music

Stravinsky once described *Oedipus* as a "*Merzbild*, put together from whatever came to hand".[3] Stately dotted rhythms, reminiscent of Bach, accompany Oedipus early on, while an Alberti bass heralds the entrance of the Messenger. From such bits and pieces of Baroque and Classical cliché a unity is forged, however, and the glue that holds this assortment together consists often enough of features that are typical of Stravinsky's music, regardless of the stylistic orientation.

Consider the music of the Messenger and Shepherd, an excerpt of which appears in example 12.1. The passage could easily have been lifted from any number of Russian-period works. A melodic fragment, modal in character, is sliced up into short segments by changing bar lines. Typical of the composer, the shifting bar lines ensure that the repetition of the melody, beginning at rehearsal no.140 in example 12.1, will enter at a location that is metrically parallel to the original. Both the melody and its repetition enter on the second eighth-note beat of a 3/8 measure.

EXAMPLE 12.1: *Oedipus Rex; metrical displacement (concealed)*

No less typical of the composer, however, the shifting bar lines conceal a metrical displacement. The listener could just as easily have inferred a steady 3/4 meter from this passage, according to which the repetition would be heard as metrically displaced. The brackets above the musical quotation in example 12.1 outline the 1-2-3 count of the 3/4 meter. The melody falls first on and then off the quarter-note beat. Eventually, however, as can be seen in example 12.1, the shifting bar lines are replaced by the 3/4 meter that lies to the background of the initial conception. And it is, as always, the conflict between the two forces, meter and metrical displacement, that leads to a sense of metrical disruption.

The Messenger/Shepherd passages lead directly to the lengthy section quoted in example 12.2. This is another stratification. There are five superimposed layers, each consisting of the repetition of a single triad, dyad, or motive that is fixed in its register and instrumentation. Unusually, however, there is no polyrhythm. The spans separating the repetition in all five layers total three or six quarter-note beats, all very much in synchrony with the 3/4 meter.

Neoclassicism (II): High Watermarks | 131

Consequently, there are no metrical displacements either. Alignment is fixed throughout.

EXAMPLE 12.2: *Oedipus Rex; stratification*

The vast immobility of this music carries a dramatic purpose. We have arrived, following the final departure of the Messenger and

Shepherd at rehearsal no.166, at the high point of the opera/oratorio: nos.167-69 coincide with Oedipus's recognition of guilt, no.169, the "*Lux facta est!*"cadence, with his final resignation. Both musically and dramatically, then, rehearsal nos.167-70 represent a period of waiting and anticipation, a pause to digest. For the main character, it is a moment of appalling humbling.

Register, instrumentation, rhythm, and meter are not the only means of stasis at this point in the drama. Pitch is a means as well. In example 12.2, the five superimposed layers, consisting, in order of appearance, of (D F A), (D F#), B-F#, (D F), and (F# B D), are all subject to the symmetries of the octatonic scale: in ascending order, D-Eb-F-F#-G#-A-B-C-(D). Only the pitch C#, a passing tone in Oedipus' reiterating motive, lies outside the octatonic scale in question.

The Classical side to Stravinsky's neoclassical bargain in example 12.2 makes itself felt by way of three 18th-century conventions: 1) the (D F#) unit in the flutes inflects a *tierce de Picardie* in relation to the reiteration of (D F A) in the lower strings; 2) the (F# B D) triadic outline in Oedipus's motive is the submediant in relation to (D F# A); 3) the F of the (D F) unit in the clarinet clashes with B-F# in the timpani and with a (D F#) in the flutes. As we shall see in the coming chapter, the clashing of major and minor thirds would become a hallmark of the composer's late neoclassical style.

Symphony of Psalms

Episodes all but forgotten in Stravinsky's neoclassical biography are his transcriptions for the player-piano and the heavy concertizing he undertook during the 1920s and 30s. On average, at least half of each year during this period was spent in recording studios and on tour in Europe, the United States, and even South America. Most of his income derived from these sources. And he seems to have enjoyed the traveling, introducing and presenting his music to the public. As an added incentive, Vera de Bosset often accompanied him on these trips. Indeed, it appears to have been on just such a tour that Soulima and then his family first learned of Vera's existence. The family was stunned, but the extent of their acceptance over time is difficult to measure. Soulima and Theodore resigned themselves early on to the presence of another woman in their father's life. They were frequently in Paris during the 1930s, meeting up with their father at Vera's apartment.

In September of 1929, Stravinsky was approached by Koussevitzky and the Boston Symphony Orchestra about the possibility of composing a symphony to commemorate the orchestra's 50th anniversary season, 1929-30. Not until December 12, 1929 was a contract signed for $6000, and not until later that month did the first jottings appear along with the following lines from Psalm 39: "Hear my prayer, O Lord, and with thine ears consider my calling." From these early days, the new work took on the character of a choral symphony, sacred and devotional in spirit.

No sooner had the ink dried on the initial sketches, however, that Stravinsky was off on a tour in Germany, conducting *Apollo* in Berlin and appearing as soloist in the *Capriccio*. Much of February was spent in Romania and Czechoslovakia. And although March had been set aside for composition, he was soon concertizing again in Switzerland, this time in Winterthur. Nevertheless, by the end of April, most of the third movement had been completed, and Stravinsky turned next to the double fugue of the second movement. The symphony was thus written in reverse order, as the *Capriccio* had been a year earlier. While the first and second movements feature verses from Psalms 38 and 39, the third sets Psalm 150 in its entirety.

Premiered on the evening of December 13, 1930, in Brussels, with Ansermet conducting, the *Symphony of Psalms* swiftly became one of Stravinsky's most performed and popular works. Much of the music is typical of the composer: the octatonic stratifications in the first movement, and the examples of displacement, stratification, and polyrhythm in the third. Shown in example 12.3 is the first music to be composed, the opening of the Allegro in the third movement. Consisting of the reiteration of a C-major triad, the "theme" is subjected to a series of metrical displacements. (Compare this opening Allegro in *Psalms* with example 8.1 from *The Rite of Spring*.)

More specifically in example 12.3, the theme, introduced on the second quarter-note beat of a 4/4 measure, is subsequently displaced to the downbeat and then the fourth beat. Working against these shifts in alignment, however, all other features of the theme are retained from one repetition to the next. (This is true even of the theme's articulation and its opening *sforzando*.) The retention of these features intensifies the listener's expectations of metrical parallelism, that the theme will be repeated at the original metrical location. The irreconcilable nature of these two conflicting forces, displacement and parallelism, is apt to prove disruptive of the listener's sense of the 4/4 meter.

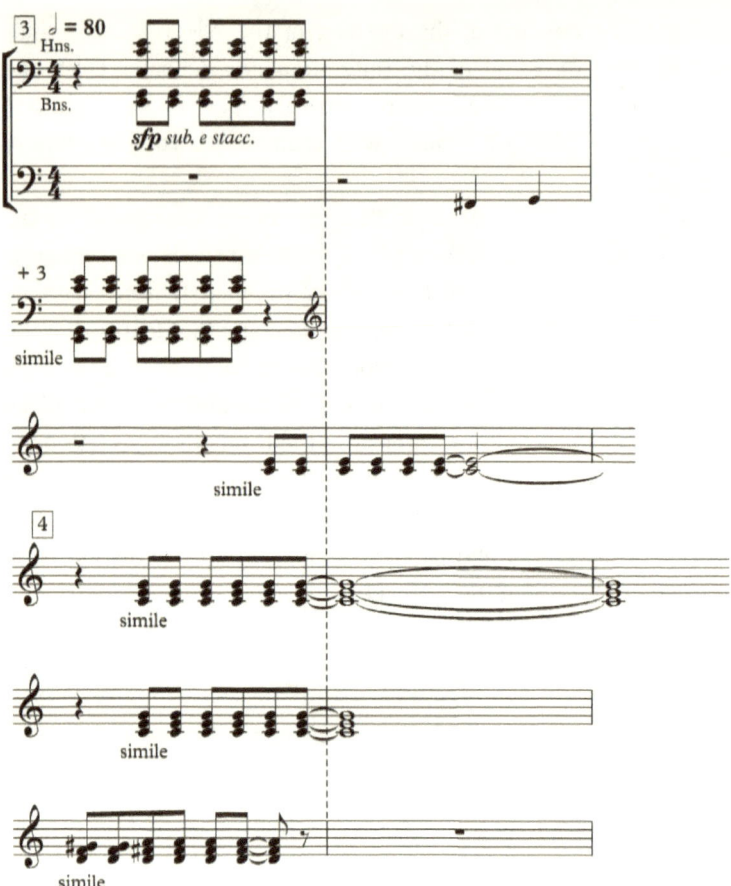

EXAMPLE 12.3: *Symphony of Psalms* (1930), III, opening bars; metrical displacement

The third movement of *Psalms* ends with an apotheosis; see example 12.4. Quietly, the repetition of a melody in the chorus is superimposed polyrhythmically over an ostinato pattern of four quarter-note beats. The final chord features a *tierce de Picardie*, more specifically, the E-natural of a C-major triad. The *tierce* intones a single word, Dominum (God); "Let there be light," as it were. The word is cut up rather badly in *Psalms*, but the dissection serves Stravinsky's rhythmic purposes, the manner of his "versification."

EXAMPLE 12.4: *Symphony of Psalms, III; apotheosis stratification*

The beauty of these concluding pages of *Psalms* is doubtless reflective of the particular circumstances surrounding their conception, textual as well as musical. Yet the idea of an apotheosis is not new in Stravinsky's music, as it appears at the end of both *The Wedding* and *Apollo*—Russian and neoclassical works, respectively, which in other ways could not be more distant from one another. A plateau is reached in each of these instances, a stoppage of harmonic rhythm or movement; a configuration or motive is repeated insistently as a kind of refrain. The effect is mysterious and otherworldly; the music "floats," as Stephen Walsh has suggested, "as if in defiance of tonal and rhythmic gravity." There is a religious or at least spiritual dimension to these conditions at the close of *Psalms*, one that can seem intensely worshipful in tone. The Lord is praised again and again in the six verses of Psalm 150, praised in his "greatness," "goodness," and "glory," as the inscription on the composer's dedication page reminds us. The first movement, the last of the three to be composed, was completed in a "state of religious exultation," as the composer claimed later in *Dialogues and a Diary*.

For Stravinsky, the canons of the Christian Church embodied a form of absolute truth, one that was to be summoned daily as part of an orderly existence. Such was the ideal, in any case, cherished and even practiced to a degree during the neoclassical years of the 1920s and 30s in France, and then later in California as well. Nearly all of Stravinsky's late 12-tone music was set to sacred texts of one kind or another.

13. Neoclassicism (III): Late Years

We meet up with Stravinsky again in April of 1939 at the Sancellemoz sanatorium in the Haute Savoie region of France, close to the Swiss border. Both his second-born and wife have died of tuberculosis—Mika in November of 1938 and Katya on March 2, 1939. He himself has been recovering from a relapse of this disease, and will be staying on at Sancellemoz for another month or two as an outpatient. Professionally, he has just accepted an invitation from the Music Department at Harvard to deliver the Charles Eliot Norton lectures during the 1939-40 academic year.

His acceptance of this lecture-proposal (quickly, within two weeks) is puzzling at first blush. He is the first musician to be honored in this way, to be sure, but he will also be having to leave France ("home"), and to lecture and teach a class in composition. Earlier, in 1935-37, he had taught a composition course under the auspices of the Ecole Normale de Musique with the celebrated pedagogue and musician Nadia Boulanger, but as a rule, these were not the sorts of activities to which he was accustomed or even attracted. Yet he would persevere, possibly for the following reasons: 1) at $10,000, the invitation was another offer too generous to refuse, and 2) given the recent calamities that had befallen him, the idea of leaving France for an extended period may have appealed to him. He would also be arranging for a concert tour of five or so American cities starting in October of 1939 and ending in May of the following year.

While at Sancellemoz, Stravinsky had already begun preparing for the lectures, consulting with the philosopher Pierre Souvtchinsky and hiring Alexis Roland-Manuel, a writer and protégé of Ravel's, to do the actual writing. Just as with the earlier *Autobiography*, the six lectures will be ghostwritten. (In further negotiations with his hosts,

Stravinsky had managed to whittle the eight lectures down to six, and to augment his stipend to $12,000.)

All of which is not to imply that the lectures would not ultimately be "his," that they would not reflect his ideas on a range of musical topics. Souvtchinsky, a long-time friend and intimately familiar with the composer's ideas on a host of musical and aesthetic issues, will be contributing the fifth lecture, focusing on Russian music; his Russian will be translated into French by the composer's son, Soulima. Roland-Manuel will be working primarily from interviews and a 19-page outline that the composer had written out while still in Sancellemoz.[1]

Of course, the impeccable French will not be Stravinsky's. The composer's French, spoken and written, was far from perfect. Yet it was as a composer that he would continue to resist the heavy lifting, as it were, pleading the necessity of devoting as much time as possible to composition.

A practice reading of at least one of the lectures was held at Boulanger's apartment in Paris, apparently on the eve of Stravinsky's departure for America. Also present was the critic and poet Paul Valery, a friend of the composer's and, as it now appears, the source of some of the aesthetic ideals expressed in the lectures. Indeed, there were other literary figures, including André Gide and Jacques Maritain, whose writings appear to have played a role in the thinking of both Stravinsky and Roland-Manuel.[2]

On the Harvard campus in October 1939, the first of Stravinsky's lectures was as much a social event as a musical or academic one. In tails, Koussevitsky attended, as did many adoring members of his Boston Symphony audiences. The last to enter the lecture hall was Stravinsky himself, also in tails, bowing steeply to Edward Forbes, his host at the Harvard Music Department. The composer was not exceedingly nervous, only conspicuously unfamiliar with the protocol. The mood was festive and welcoming all the same, and he was warmly received both before and after the reading. However, the chances are surely slim that his ideas about musical time, composition, Russian music, and performance practice, delivered in

Roland-Manuel's academic French, had been understood by more than a dozen or so in attendance.

Stravinsky's remaining five lectures were spread over the academic year. By the time of the last lecture on April 10, 1940, he had married his mistress, Vera de Bosset, and had applied for an extension of his temporary visa, evidently with the intention of becoming a U.S. citizen. He had left France in September of the previous year with a return ticket in hand, but the war had gradually eliminated any such prospect.

An English translation of the composer's lectures appeared in 1947 under the title of *Poetics of Music in the Form of Six Lessons*. Now in their 16th edition, the "lessons" have been widely read and discussed, notwithstanding the substance and style, which is often stiff and off-putting. The sixth "lesson" repeats the composer's arguments in favor of a strict performing practice, only a bit more tyrannically than on earlier occasions.

Beginning in 1959, Stravinsky would go on to co-author six books of "conversation," interviews, and diaries with his associate, Robert Craft. He would claim that the picture that emerged of him in these later books was a good deal more authentic or "like him" than anything the earlier volumes had managed to convey. But the problem here again is that these later books, too, were mostly ghostwritten. Stravinsky would sometimes tinker with the final drafts, as Craft reported in 2006, adding or subtracting here and there. (The composer enjoyed typing as a form of relaxation.) But the images of him were mostly Craft's, and it was Craft's literary imagination that lay at the heart of these endeavors.

But even autobiography may be reckoned as a form of impersonation, and it seems safe to assume that the first three books of the series, *Conversations with Stravinsky* (1959), *Memories and Commentaries* (1961), and *Expositions and Developments* (1962), bring readers about as close to Stravinsky the person as they are likely to get. Many of Craft's accounts of Stravinsky's compositional processes, his manner of conducting, musical personality, and daily routines are unforgettable, and comprise a treasure worth exploring by all enthusiasts of his music.

This applies to no less an extent to Craft's later biography, *Chronicle of a Friendship* (1972). In the 1960s, he and Stravinsky began publishing articles and interviews in the popular press, including the *New York Review of Books*. The two became public figures after a fashion, in demand for comments on a variety of subjects, by no means exclusively musical. President Kennedy held a dinner at the White House in honor of the composer's 80th birthday. The stimulus for this celebration appears to have come from the president's wife, Jacqueline, who, as an undergraduate at Vassar, had made a study of Diaghilev and the early years of the Ballets Russes. Later in 1964, the composer would write a short 12-tone memorial for the President, *Elegy for JFK*, which Craft conducted in Los Angeles on April 6, 1964.

Nadia Boulanger, teacher *extraordinaire*

Vera de Bosset was not alone in following Stravinsky to America before and after the outbreak of WWII. Nadia Boulanger did so as well, arriving in New York from Lisbon on November 5, 1940.[3] Her role as an early champion of the composer's neoclassical music is an interesting one.

On close personal and professional terms with Stravinsky for many years, Boulanger conducted and performed at the piano. In September of 1938, she conducted the first performance of Stravinsky's "Dumbarton Oaks" Concerto in E-flat. But she was first and foremost a teacher, an instructor *extraordinaire* in the practical skills of being a musician. She taught these fundamentals primarily to young composers, often American, and became famous doing so. Yet she taught many performers as well, especially pianists. Among her early students were Aaron Copland, Virgil Thomson, Roy Harris, and Soulima Stravinsky. (Soulima was sent to Paris to study music theory with Boulanger in October of 1929.) Although her advice to young composers was doubtless invaluable, much of what she taught transcended these categories. Above all, she taught phrasing, the art of breathing and articulating music. And like Stravinsky, she was a despot when it came to the necessity of maintaining an even beat.

Depending on the age of a student and the length of her stay, Boulanger often began with keyboard harmony—more precisely, Paul Vidal's swarm of figured basses. Her students were required to realize these basses in writing, with each of the four parts assigned its own staff, the latter to allow the musical logic of each to make itself felt. Each part would also be assigned its own clef, which meant, reading from top to bottom, the soprano, alto, tenor, and bass clefs. ("Mademoiselle," as she was known to just about everyone, would not read exercises which had not been phrased properly.) Students would then play the figured basses at the piano in different keys, singing the individual parts as they went along. Graduates of this regimen knew a great deal about the parts of a Classical-era string quartet or symphony. After Vidal, came Theodore Dubois' *Traite de l'Harmonie*, with its unfigured basses and given melodies or *Chants donnés*. DuBois might be followed by counterpoint and/or orchestration.

Unlike Stravinsky, Boulanger returned to Paris after the war, resettling in her large apartment in the rue Ballu, a long, narrow street connecting the rue de Clichy with the rue Blanche. (These two arteries connect the Boulevard de Clichy with the Trinité church down the hill.) From morning to night, she would sit at the piano with her students reading through exercises, scores, and so forth. Like Rimsky-Korsakov, Boulanger held her *jours fixes* (musical gatherings) on Wednesdays, although in the afternoon rather than the evening. Close to 2 PM, her students (including the author, who studied with her during the 1960s), would gather on the wide, marble staircase leading up to her apartment on the second floor. Filing in, one or two students would occupy the piano (often ex-students, or notables of one kind or another), Boulanger would lecture and conduct, and the remainder of the flock would comprise a chorus of sorts.

Mademoiselle assigned music for each Wednesday: Bach cantatas too numerous to mention here (among her favorites were No.8, "Liebster Gott, wann werd'ich sterben?," and No.105, "Herr, gehe nicht ins Gericht"); selections from Bach's *Orgelbuchlein*; Mozart's String Quintet in G minor; Hindemith's *Das Marienleben* (original version); Stravinsky's *Capriccio*, and other neoclassical works. She soldiered on with Stravinsky's 12-tone pieces, including *Threni* (1958) and *A Sermon, a Narrative, and a Prayer* (1961), insisting all along—unpersuasively, as it seemed at the time—that every note remained Stravinsky's alone. During a two-and-half-year period, she assigned not a single work of the late Romantics. The fact that, since the early 1950s, the neoclassical music she promoted had fallen out of favor with the serious compositional crowd did not affect her purpose or enthusiasm for a moment. It was as if the other side—the Schoenberg-Webern-Berg side and, later, the integral serialism of Pierre Boulez—had scarcely existed.

Occasionally, Boulanger's class would rehearse for a concert at the Princess de Polignac's salon, site of so many programs and trial runs of Stravinsky's works. The violinist Yehudi Menuhin, another close friend of Boulanger's, would sometimes play a Bach Partita. Copland came to Paris in the early spring of 1964, to conduct the orchestral version of his *Piano Variations* (1930), which had only recently been completed. After the concert, Boulanger held a reception in her apartment for Copland, Virgil Thomson, and her students.

These experiences were close to ordinary at the time, the participants and circumstances not having assumed the near-mythical status that lay ahead by a few decades. Similarly, in Paris itself, the sand-blasting of the city's architecture had only just begun, and most neighborhoods remained as they doubtless had been for centuries: gray, dirty, cold, blackened, and grim. A glittering plaything it was not, a city with fewer people than today, a good deal less wealth, and an orientation that was decidedly regional rather than global. Paradoxically, however, much more seemed possible then. The cafés, boulevards, cobblestones, and *pissoires* (public urinals) were characteristic and knowable. You could touch Paris, a thing distinct and set apart, no matter the rootedness, the tentacles that stretched everywhere and were in everything.

"Journeyman's jobs"

In early April 1941, not long after settling with Vera into his new home on North Wetherly Drive in Hollywood, the composer began turning to what he called "journeyman's jobs"–commissions he would not have accepted if his income in Europe had not been curtailed by the war. Included among these "jazz commercials" (Craft's term) were the *Circus Polka* (1942) and the *Scherzo à la russe* (1944), composed for the Ringling Brothers' Circus and Paul Whiteman's band, respectively. The *Ebony Concerto* (1945) was written for Woody Herman's instrumentation, to which the composer added a French horn.

No less out of the ordinary, Stravinsky began to teach. His student, Earnest Andersson, a wealthy, retired inventor, brought with him the beginnings of a four-movement symphony which he wished to complete under Stravinsky's supervision. Starting in January of 1941, he and Stravinsky collaborated on this *Futurama* symphony for about a year. Remarkably, Stravinsky seems to have taught Andersson what Rimsky-Korsakov had taught him decades earlier in St. Petersburg: orchestration and octatonic harmony. In the first movement of the *Futurama* symphony, as transcribed and published by Colin Slim[4], the dominant-seventh chords, octatonically related, mirror those in *The Rite of Spring*; they appear in first inversion and are confined to the octave. And the mirroring was no accident. *The Rite* was very much in the air at the time, given the success of Walt Disney's *Fantasia* (1940), for which, of course, Stravinsky had provided the accompaniment. (More than an accompaniment, the rhythms of his ballet score had inspired much of the movement in Disney's animated film.)

More remarkably still, Stravinsky's teaching had an impact on his own composition. During the 1930s, in pieces such as the Violin Concerto (1931), the *Concerto for Two Pianos* (1935), and *Jeux de Cartes* (1937), the octatonic scale had figured scarcely if at all. Beginning with a number of passages in *Danses Concertantes* (1942), however, all this changed. The *Symphony in Three Movements* (1945), begun in 1942, marks the composer's most extensive use of octatonic harmony since the *Symphony of Psalms*.

The opening theme of the new symphony, wholly octatonic in terms of the pitches (Db E F G Ab Bb), is superimposed over rising C-major scales in the bass. And the lengthy section that follows at Rehearsal nos. 7-13, no less octatonic, features an exchange of dominant sevenths superimposed over an A-C-A basso ostinato.

While the orientation of this material is neoclassical, the loud, brash sound of the orchestra can remind the listener of the earlier Russian-period ballet scores.

The second movement of the *Symphony in Three Movements*, Andante, originated as a film project. As a means of boosting his income, the composer had long cherished the hope of composing for the cinema. And he might have succeeded in this quest had the financial and artistic arrangements, as he later complained, not been "so entirely in favor of the film producers".[5] Parts of the Andante were originally designed to accompany scenes in a film by Franz Werfel, *Song of Bernadette*. The film was later released by 20th Century Fox, but with the music of another composer, Alfred Newman.

As a form of accompaniment, the repetition of the dyad F#/D with which the Andante begins is typically Classical; see example 13.1. What happens in the lower strings in the first two measures is typical of Stravinsky, however; an F-natural, pizzicato, is made to clash with the F# or major third of the tonic triad (D F# A). Exhibited in this way is a form of "major-minor emphasis," according to which the minor third is brought into conflict with the major third of a tonic triad.

EXAMPLE 13.1: *Symphony in Three Movements, II, opening bars*

The rapid figuration in the flutes further along at rehearsal no.117 yields a content of (D F F# G# A B), a transposition of the opening theme of the first movement. Here, F-natural and G# serve alternatively as chromatic tendency tones to F# and A, respectively, the major third and fifth of the tonic triad. This is the traditional, tonal, and expressive use to which these chromatic pitches are put in the music of Haydn, Mozart, and Beethoven.

The diagram on the top staff of example 13.2 can further illuminate the Classical side of Stravinsky's neoclassical bargain. The three stems connected by a beam outline the tonic triad (D F# A); F-natural, G#, and B, forming a diminished triad, *embellish* the chord tones of that triad. This is their traditional, tonal, and expressive use, as we have indicated. In Stravinsky's Andante, however, with F-natural clashing with the chord tone F#, elements that might earlier have succeeded one another expressively, are now statically superimposed. The origin of this superimposition may be traced to the interacting octatonic scale shown on the bottom staff in example 13.3. In short, the (D F F# G# A D) content, with its symmetrically defined (D F F#) (F F# A) major-minor third groupings, is as octatonic in conception as it is accountable to the D-major tonality.

EXAMPLE 13.2: *D-major and octatonic scales*

Among the many neoclassical contexts that relate closely to the interacting octatonic-diatonic circumstances outlined in example nos.13.1 and 2, see rehearsal nos.30-34 in *Danses Concertantes* (1942), *Babel* (1944), the first movement of the "Basle" String Concerto in D (1946), and the "Air de danse" and "Pas des furies" in *Orpheus* (1947). Ultimately, however, the origin of these major and minor thirds may be traced back to the fugato theme in the variation movement of the *Octet*.

14. The Serial Period

I have had to survive two crisis as a composer, though as I continued to move from work to work I was not aware of either of them as such, or, indeed, of any momentous change. The first—the loss of Russia and its language of words as well as of music—affected every circumstance of my personal no less than my artistic life. Crisis number two was brought on by the musical outgrowing of the special incubator in which I wrote *The Rake's Progress* (1948-51). [Igor Stravinsky and Robert Craft, *Themes and Episodes*.]

When [Robert Craft] moved there in 1948, Los Angeles was divided like the rest of the musical world into twin hegemonies of Stravinsky and Schoenberg. The dividing was Los Angeles's and the world's doing, of course, not the two master's: divisions meant little to them in their search for that humility that is the perfect knowledge of one's art. The fact remains: they were kept separate and isolated. Paris and Vienna had crossed the world with them, re-establishing small and exceedingly provincial Viennas and Parises separated by only ten miles of Hollywood no-man's land, but as far apart as ever. Musicians came from all over the world to visit them, not mentioning to one composer their meetings with the other one. [Robert Craft, "A Personal Preface".]

Change of Life

And so we arrive at the juncture of another "change of life," a shift in musical orientation: Stravinsky's adoption of 20th-century serial techniques. Coming on the heels of his opera *The Rake's Progress* (1948-51), the first signs of a move in this direction seem to have taken just about everyone by surprise. And well might this have been the case. For the 18th-century Classical credentials of *The Rake* are formidable. Inspired initially by a series of William Hogarth's engravings (on exhibit at the Chicago Art Institute in 1947), graced by an exquisite libretto authored jointly by W. H. Auden and Chester Kallman, *The Rake* is in fact closely modeled after Mozart. We have it from both Stravinsky and Robert Craft that recordings of *Cosi fan tutte* were a daily routine at the time of *The Rake*'s inception and composition. And Craft added that Stravinsky habitually limited his "musical intake" when occupied with composition, "listening only to those pieces which he regards as directional to his work".[1]

At the same time, there existed the Schoenberg-Stravinsky rift to which the music world had long accustomed itself. This divide bore the earmarks of a rivalry of opposing camps, as we have remarked already: one aligned with the music and ideas of Schoenberg and his students Webern and Berg, and the other still seeking and finding in Stravinsky's neoclassical modes of accommodation an alternative to "the method of composing with twelve tones." Craft's contention (see above) was that these "hegemonies" were in large part the creation of the Musical Establishment, and that, as the Vienna-Paris split between Schoenberg and Stravinsky shrank to a 10-mile radius of Hollywood, the division meant little to the trapped "protagonists." The two composers "were kept separate and isolated." (Schoenberg and his family had fled Nazi Germany in 1933, traveling first to Paris and Boston before settling in Los Angeles a year or so later.)

Surely there was more to the rivalry than this. Stravinsky listened enthusiastically to Schoenberg's *Pierrot lunaire* while on a visit to Berlin with Diaghilev in December 1912. But although, in his later recollection, this early encounter was "the most prescient confrontation in my life," it was quickly forgotten, as he turned to the stimulus of Russian popular verse, and then, circa 1919, to his "discovery of the past" in *Pulcinella*. He was present at the 1925 ISCM World Music Days Festival in Venice to perform his *Piano Sonata*, but missed Schoenberg's *Serenade*. He also missed the Paris premiere of Schoenberg's *Five Pieces for Orchestra* in 1922, and the world premiere of the *Suite*, opus 29, in Paris in 1927. There was doubtless an element of self-protection in all this. Convinced of the validity of his claim and of its continuing potential, he may not have wished to be distracted.

But how to explain the 10 years of proximity within "the City and County of Los Angeles?" Why should these composers, approaching or within the twilight of their careers, so stubbornly have kept their distance from each other, shunning even the most perfunctory acquaintance? (Stravinsky might well have acquiesced. Professionally and artistically the more secure, he was the less lonely, the less neglected or abused of the two.) Both composers were present at Franz Werfel's funeral in August of 1945, and then again at a concert honoring Schoenberg in October 1949. They kept to themselves, however, shying away even from the pleasantries of an informal exchange.

Stravinsky and Craft

And so to what might Stravinsky's final "change of life" have been owing? Was it perhaps that he stirred, his "rare form of kleptomania" sprung to life, only when tempted by the music of dead composers? Did Schoenberg's death on July 13, 1951, suddenly bracket the serial advance with a historical legitimacy, a sense of tradition which it could not have had with its founding father still alive? (Removing, at the same time, the potentially crippling handicap of an all-too-knowing, watchful ear?) Or were the origins of Stravinsky's serialism more direct and specifically musical? Could *The Rake*, three years in the making, have exhausted the neoclassical palate, leaving Stravinsky restless and increasingly eager to strike out from this terrain?

And what might Craft's role have been in this miraculous flip-flop? Something other than a guide? For a long while, the confidant denied all responsibility: "As if anyone," he mused, "could have led *that* horse to water if he didn't want to go, let alone make it drink".[2] Craft would change his mind, however. In a lecture in 1998 at the Morgan Library in New York, he asked whether, without him, Stravinsky would have developed a form of serialism. His answer: "I am certain he would not have".[3]

The two first met on the morning of March 31, 1948, at a hotel in Washington D.C. Just 23 and already a brilliant musician and writer, Craft had been anxious to iron out the arrangements of an upcoming concert with Stravinsky in New York. The fatefulness of this encounter would play itself out in more ways than one. On that same day, W. H. Auden arrived with the completed libretto of *The Rake* in hand. ("Easily the quickest mind and wit" among Stravinsky's friends and colleagues, Auden was also "the most eccentric," as Craft remembered him in *Down a Path of Wonder*, 2006.) Intermittently, all three—Craft, Auden, and Stravinsky—would be in close contact in the years leading up to the premiere of *The Rake* in Venice on September 11, 1951.

Later in 1948, Craft was put to work sorting out boxes and crates of music and manuscripts at Stravinsky's home in Hollywood. But he helped with the composition of *The Rake's Progress* as well, especially where Auden's libretto was concerned. He was often asked to read Auden's lines aloud, repeatedly, and at varying speeds. The composer would memorize them, line by line or by couplet, repeating them while paying close attention (as always) to the syllables and their sounds. In accord with his understanding of the accentuation, Stravinsky would then notate the rhythms by beaming note-heads together in various ways just above Auden's words and syllables. In the process, intervals of melody and harmony would suggest themselves. Much of *The Rake* was conceived in this fashion, very nearly with the text and rhythm preceding pitch.

But it was as a conductor of contemporary music that Craft's usefulness would be felt first and foremost. Following performances of *The Rake* in 1951, he and Stravinsky turned in earnest to the music of Schoenberg, Webern, and Berg, studying the scores and listening to the recordings. In January and February of 1952, Stravinsky attended all 20 rehearsals of Craft conducting Schoenberg *Suite*, opus 29, at the University of Southern California. Later that year, with score in hand, he attended at least as many rehearsals and studio sessions when Craft recorded the *Suite*. Like many of Schoenberg's 12-tone works, the *Suite* is neoclassical (even neo-baroque) in its larger forms, phrases, and thematic types. Yet the musical language is 12-tone and hence thoroughly "dissonant"–thoroughly weaned from "the shackles of tonality." What struck Stravinsky at the time was the *Suite's* instrumental virtuosity and the "constructive logic" of the serial application.

Serial conversion

In the end, then, a host of factors may have contributed to Stravinsky's serial conversion. Each of the entries mentioned above may have figured in one way or another. The question, however, is why Stravinsky, more specifically as a composer, should have turned from the start not to Schoenberg (founder of the 12-tone method), but rather to Schoenberg's pupil Webern–that member of the Viennese trio who had so completely divested himself of the rhetoric which neoclassicism had sought to reclaim. Indeed, that member who, by so divesting himself, had bequeathed the serial camp a new sense of musical timing and space.

We may grant the cool, detached manner of Webern's musical intensity, the leanness and transparency of texture that would in any event have met with a sympathetic ear. It would not be long before Stravinsky would be complaining about the "radically alien emotional climate" of Berg's music[4], and the melodramatic, *fin-de-siècle* pathos of so much of Schoenberg's. Familiar with all of Schoenberg's music by the late 1950s, he would admit to an aesthetic attraction only to *Pierrot lunaire* and the *Serenade*. (Imagine! This was the very *Serenade* whose performance in 1925 in Venice, with Schoenberg conducting, he had deliberately avoided.

But he was now likening the spirit of Schoenberg's *Serenade* to that of his own *Soldier's Tale*!)

More damming still, Stravinsky thought nearly all of Schoenberg's texts "appallingly bad," overwrought and dated, in essence, "as to discourage performance of the music." To put this further in perspective: Stravinsky was now attending rehearsals of Webern's works, all 31 of which were in the process of being recorded by Craft for Columbia records.

But there is occasion for greater specificity here. Stravinsky may have been attracted to the symmetry of Webern's 12-tone rows, the segmental patterning by which this symmetry exposes itself. He may have found in the segmentation, in the major-minor third units, familiar grounds from which to depart. Just as neoclassicism can sometimes be heard and understood as a form of accommodation between octatonic harmony and the conventions of Baroque and Classical tonality, so, too, the early serial stage of the 1950s can often be reckoned as an imposition of a formalized serial mechanism on an existent articulative mold.

Such would seem to be the case were we to compare the serial rows in Example 14.1. In the two rows from Webern's *Concerto* and *Variations*, successions of major and minor thirds abound, and with the rows so deployed as to afford these groupings a quite unmistakable measure of articulative cohesion. The 12-tone row of the *Concerto* divides into four three-note segments (see the vertical dotted lines), each of these a transposition and then an inversion and/or retrograde of the initial unit, B-Bb-D. The major and minor thirds of the latter are Bb-D and B-D.

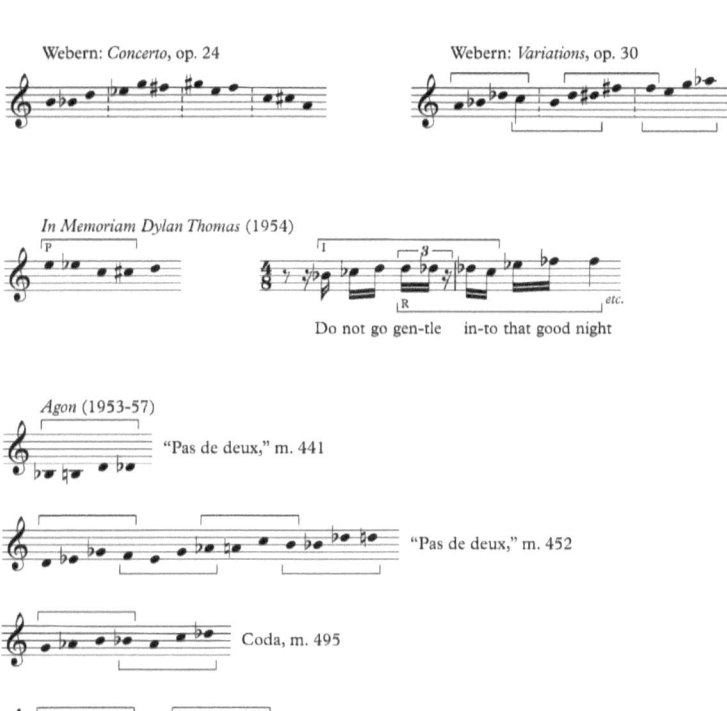

EXAMPLE 14.1: *Early row forms*

In the *Variations*, the row's segmentation is more readily tripartite, with the initial tetrachordal unit in terms of A-Bb-Db-C having as its retrograde inversion the concluding segment, F-E-G-Ab. Transposed or transformed, the latter tetrachord dominates the serial application not only in Stravinsky's *In Memoriam Dylan Thomas* (1954), but in several sections of *Agon* as well: "Pas de due", Coda, and the "Four Trios." Notice, in example 14.1, the overlapping of successive tetrachords in *Agon*, with the last pitch of one becoming the first of the next. This, too, is a borrowing from the row of Webern's *Variations*.

But the significance of this current tetrachord extends far beyond the serial rows in *Agon*. Like the Dorian tetrachord cited earlier

The Serial Period | 155

in connection with Stravinsky's Russian-period works, the present one is a segment of the octatonic scale. And it appears as such in manifold neoclassical contexts, although perhaps especially in the *Symphony of Psalms*, where it functions as "the root idea of the whole work," as Stravinsky himself coined it in 1963. He further described its use in *Psalms* as consisting of "two minor thirds joined by a major third".[5]

The excerpts shown in example 14.2 are from the highly octatonic first movement of *Psalms*. At rehearsal no.7, the accompaniment in this stratified texture consists of the superimposition of tritone-related tetrachords, conceived as ostinatos in the oboes and lower strings. Shown below is the octatonic scale to which this articulation relates.

EXAMPLE 14.2: *Symphony of Psalms*, I, octatonic stratifications

In the second movement of *Psalms* the same tetrachord appears as a segment of the C-minor scale (the harmonic minor). Shown in example 14.3, the tetrachord appears as the opening of a fugal subject, C-Eb-B-D. Not only is this articulation a neoclassical form of interaction between the octatonic scale and the tonal. The tetrachord would persevere in Stravinsky's early serial works.

EXAMPLE 14.3: *Symphony of Psalms, II, fugue subject*

Canticum Sacrum

Bleak and stern, without cheer and very nearly without "play," Stravinsky's *Canticum Sacrum* (1955) is of a world far removed from the sophisticated dazzle of *Agon*. A few clues do suggest its sandwiched position between the non-serial beginnings and serial completion of the ballet. The Bb-Db reiteration in the bass pattern of the first movement, joined by a D-B span and an occasional (G B D) triad in the chorus and brass brings *Agon's* Prelude and Interlude to mind. And there is unmistakably a touch of the Stravinskian dance in the first movement, if only by virtue of a fiendishly tricky dotted quarter-note: although placed off the beat, this dotted quarter is more readily heard and understood on the beat, with succeeding measures encumbered by an off-the-beat stagger.

The gravity in mood has ultimately to do with belief, and belief evidently profoundly institutional in spirit. Stressed above all is the issue of faith and the trials of the fallen, themes which would find expression in a host of biblical and liturgical texts, the lamentations of Jeremiah (*Threni*, 1955), the stoning of Stephen (*A Sermon, a Narrative, and a Prayer*, 1961), the saga of Noah (*The Flood*, 1962), and the sacrifice of Abraham (*Abraham and Isaac*, 1964). The *Symphony of Psalms* and the *Mass* may be cited as forerunners. But the general climate is nonetheless increasingly characteristic of the serial period. *Agon* would be followed by *Movements* (1959) and the

Variations for orchestra (1964). But *Canticum* would host a more plentiful lot: in addition to the four works just cited, *Introius* (1965) and the *Requiem Canticles* (1966), were among the very latest of the late.

Commissioned by the Venice Biennial Festival of Contemporary Music, *Canticum* is dedicated to Venice and its Patron Saint, "the Blessed Mark, Apostle." The premiere was in fact held at Saint Mark's Cathedral on September 13, 1955, a circumstance which is now felt to have influenced features of the score. The five domes of the cathedral may have inspired the five movements, with the lengthy middle movement in three parts symbolic of the cathedral's central dome. The orchestra is quasi-Venetian, with its four trumpets, four trombones (including bass and contrabass), and its scattering of oboes and bassoons. There are no violins or cellos, only violas and double basses.

While the "Surge, aquilo" section of the second movement is 12-tone, the first and last movements are nonserial. The latter are true flanking movements, and are bound as such in a most unusual fashion: the last is a nearly literal retrograde of the first. This may not be immediately discernible, the listener merely sensing in the final movement something of continuation and conclusion. As might be expected, it is in these nonserial boundary movements of *Canticum* that the Stravinsky of the past, of whatever stylistic persuasion, is most readily apparent.

Two blocks are placed in juxtaposition with one another, yielding an overall A B A B A structure. The first of these blocks is densely scored for full orchestra and chorus, the second for organ with bassoons doubling the bass line. The referential implications of the scheme are of special note: the initial *tutti* block is octatonic-diatonic in conception, while the organ block is diatonic, implying the Dorian mode.

The octatonicism of the first block is fairly routine. Spaced between the soprano's D and a low Bb is the (Bb B D) major-minor third unit, stressed as a succession in the chorus, and then verticalized massively in the organ. Octatonic triads rooted on E, G, and Bb are outlined in the trumpets and a trombone. Superimposed, however, these triads are obscured, and it is the (Bb B D) unit and the clashing of its major and minor thirds, (Bb D) and (B D), that take precedence.

By the early 1960s, the composer had declared himself a more serial composer than ever, as well as the inventor of new ways of creating row forms. Major works of this late period apply a rotation scheme to the hexachord of the 12-tone rows. In example 14.4 from *The Flood* (1962), the first hexachord of this work's prime form (on top) is followed by five rotations or "alternates." Starting with a common set-factor, G#, the rotation proceeds by interval order in the manner indicated by the diagonal lines; the first rotation begins with the second interval of the original hexachord, and it completes its cycle by reaching the original's first interval; the second rotation then begins with the original's third interval; and so forth. On the vertical axis in example 14.4, the composer reserved the six "verticals" (as he called them), starting with single pitch G#, specifically for chords or "harmonies." In shorter works of this period, Stravinsky confined himself to the untransposed forms of the row. Yet he seems to have regarded the hexachordal rotation scheme outlined in the example 14.4 as an outgrowth of compositional ends that were uniquely his.

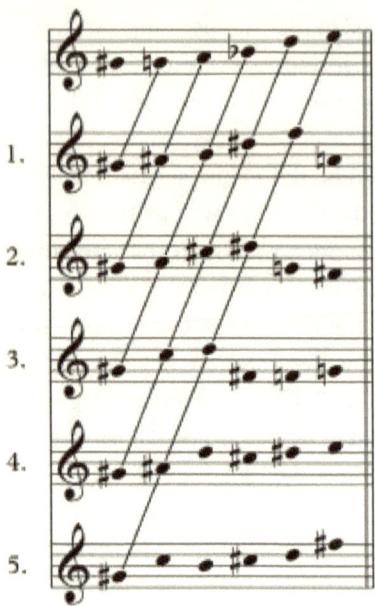

EXAMPLE 14.4: *The Flood*, hexachordal rotation

Battles over the inheritance

From 1948 until Stravinsky's death of heart failure on April 6, 1971, Craft was the composer's constant companion, interpreter, and sounding-board. He rehearsed the orchestras Stravinsky conducted, whether in recording studios or on tour. And in 1956 he began conducting the first halves of Stravinsky's concerts as well. Although the composer had by then given up performing at the piano, he continued to conduct through the 1950s and into the 60s as he approached his 80th birthday. He would sometimes open a program with a short work (often the early *Fireworks*) before handing the baton over to Craft.

Untold hours were spent by these musicians listening to music and discussing it on planes, trains, and in cars. Their friendship and collaboration was not without friction, however. There were irritations and frequent disagreements about programs, interpretations, and so forth. Both were hypertense and excitable, Stravinsky even more so when he was composing. In the throes of creative thought, he moved about "like an exposed nerve," to quote from Craft's *Down a Path of Wonder*.

Still later, Craft doubted whether, without Vera, he and Stravinsky could ever have lived and worked together. While Stravinsky was moody and a non-stop worrier, periodically at war with everything and everybody, Vera was just the opposite—steady, forgiving, and adept at "smoothing things over." She and her husband conversed in Russian, she in a voice so soft that "an argument between them was an impossibility."

As an adopted son for 23 years, Craft could hardly have escaped the line of fire where the grievances of the composer's family and his older friends in Europe were concerned. The standard family lament was that Craft had kept Stravinsky "too much to himself." In Switzerland, Theodore and his wife Denise complained bitterly that Craft "had kept him from us".[5] (Exceptionally, Pierre Souvtchinsky expressed his gratitude to Craft that, in the United States, Stravinsky had been able to continue composing as he had in Europe.)

Craft would eventually plead guilty to these charges, but with the qualification that the problem lay not entirely with himself. On several occasions, he had wanted to pursue opportunities on his own, but was prevented from doing so by Stravinsky's emotion-laden notes begging him to stay. (Stravinsky seems always to have recoiled from the personal, in his relations with others as well as in music. Forced to reveal something of his intimate feelings, he did so indirectly in writing.)

When, a few days after Stravinsky's death, a memorial service was held in his honor at St. Patrick's Cathedral in New York, Vera, Craft, Balanchine, and Stravinsky's American entourage occupied one side of the aisle, while family members sat on the other. Never would this twain meet. Hardly had Stravinsky's remains been flown to Venice and interned there on the Island of San Michele (like Diaghilev's before him), that the two sides became locked in combat, as it were, in a war without end.

Stravinsky's heirs (mainly Soulima and Theodore) opened with a formal request that the materials relating to them and their mother Katya not be offered for sale, and that an inventory and full financial accounting be taken of the archives. These were reasonable requests, certainly, but the years of debilitating litigation that followed were hardly so. One claim followed another in an atmosphere of nastiness that, even considering the petty resentments of the composer's last 10 or 15 years, far exceeded anything that could have been imagined.

Vera's ownership of the autographed full score of *The Rite of Spring* gifted by her husband was challenged by Stravinsky's children, but she sold it anyway in October of 1973, for $200,000. The children promptly filed suit. But the real bone of contention was the archive itself, which consisted of more than 100 boxes of letters, contracts, programs, newspaper cuttings, and more than 200 drawers of music manuscripts and sketches. In December of 1979, the New York Surrogate's Court reached a settlement determining ownership of the estate during and after Vera's lifetime. This did little to abate the litigation, however, which dragged on even after her death on September 17, 1982, at the age of 93.

The archive was sold at long last in the summer of 1983 to the Paul Sacher Foundation, where it remains housed to this day. It sold for 3.5 million dollars. In contention early on were UCLA, the University of Texas, and, for a short while, the New York Public Library. The sale would leave the children richer, as Stephen Walsh has speculated, "but perhaps not remarkably happier."

It seems certain that Stravinsky would have approved of the Sacher Foundation as a resting place for his musical biography. Its founder, the conductor Paul Sacher, had been a friend, and had commissioned the "Basle" String Concerto in D (1946). (A jewel of the composer's late neoclassical style, the Concerto's first movement is in a league with the *Symphony in Three Movements* and *Orpheus*, while the second movement, although very much in the spirit of Tchaikovsky, opens with a bass line that could have been lifted from any number of Baroque or Classical sources.) Later, Sacher conducted the premiere of A *Sermon, a Narrative, and a Prayer* in Basel, Switzerland, in early 1962. Located on the Munster Platz, the Foundation itself has been open to musicians and scholars not only of Stravinsky and his music. Housed there as well are the archives of a great many other 20th-century composers, including those of Stravinsky's hero by the mid-1950s and early 60s, Anton Webern.

In matters pertaining to the composer's legacy, there is unfinished business. Craft's annoyance peaked again in the mid-1990s when Stravinsky's heirs, now the composer's grandchildren, refused to sponsor a critical valorum edition of the complete works. There is justification for his ire. The German publisher Barenreiter had expressed an interest in the project, and Paul Sacher had agreed to underwrite it. But Craft's scolding remarks in *Down a Path of Wonder* would not have inspired a change of heart on the part of his adversaries:

> I can only hope that the next generation will begin to appreciate the man to whom they owe their existences and their financial wellbeing. Some fraction of the three million dollars that the family heirs received from the Disney company for the use of *The Rite of Spring* in *Fantasia* (which did incalculable good for the recognition of the composer and the promotion of his music) would help toward the establishment of a corrected edition.

Craft died on November 10, 2015, leaving behind him an extraordinary career in and out of music. Linked inextricably to Stravinsky's late music, the role he performed had been put to the test: the Stravinsky music he nurtured, conducted, and sometimes premiered is seldom, if ever, performed today. Much of the world of which it was a part–the atonal-serial-12-tone world–began its decline and fall during the 1960s and 70s, as a body of literature inviting study and performance, and as a point of entry for young composers at conservatories and universities the world over. And the likelihood of a revival seems remote. The sense of this literature as a key to the future, the point on which aspects of Western art music converged, no longer prevails. There are also issues of perception or cognition. The natural order of things does not appear to be dodecaphony and an idealized equality among the 12 pitches. Instead, a form of hierarchy would seem to be favored, along with the diatonic set and arrangements of pitch related to it in some fashion. To follow the American theorist Fred Lerdahl, the gap between serialism or 12-tone composition and the way we readily hear and understand music is too wide. Crucially, our listening experiences and abilities come with "cognitive constraints".[6]

This is no reason to throw out the baby with the bathwater. Astonishing and beautiful pieces, serial or 12-tone in conception, have been written by Stravinsky, Schoenberg, Webern, and Berg; we, the listening public, would surely be better off with some of this music reclaimed. Even if, in Stravinsky's case, the rescue might include initially only the exquisite *Requiem Canticles*, the effort would be worth our while. Coupled with a corrected, annotated edition of the complete works, the benefits would soar. For enthusiasts of Stravinsky's music, we could predict a fairly bright future.

15. Stravinsky's Legacy

There are two ways of approaching Stravinsky's legacy. We can assess the extent of the public as well as professional demand for his music, and then also the nature of the influence he and his music exerted in his time and later. These are weighty concerns. The blockbuster ballet scores have remained in the limelight, as has, on occasion, the *Symphony of Psalms* and a few other of Stravinsky's works. Ballet companies pursue the ballet music from time to time, often with new choreographies, sometimes with the old ones by Balanchine. Yet the bulk of Stravinsky's music is performed incidentally if at all, a neglect that parallels that of classical music generally in the United States. In many colleges and universities, the study of Western art music, like that of Western literature, philosophy, and history, has been under siege in recent years, forced to contend with allegations of elitism, Eurocentrism, racism, and so forth. Caught up in this general hysteria, classical music is sidelined and sometimes shunned altogether in course catalogues, swept away by a tide that may no longer be reversible.

Yet there can be no denying the pronounced impact of Stravinsky's music on the music of the past century and beyond as well. Among the many innovations in instrumentation, for example, consider the role of the percussion in *The Wedding* and *The Soldier's Tale*. No longer props valued solely for their ability to produce sound effects, these instruments are now on an equal footing with the woodwinds, brass, and strings, and provide a glimpse of what was to come fairly soon and then later in the 20th century. The percussive use of the piano, harp, and string *pizzicato* in punctuating syncopations, staccatos, and the like should also be mentioned. In Stravinsky's music, the repetition of motives and chords displaced relative to the meter is often punctuated in this fashion, even if it is more generally the freeing of the repetition from fixed metrical alignment that constitutes the foreshadowing of developments that lay ahead. In *The Rite of Spring*, rhythmic motives at the outset of the "Augurs of Spring" (see the accentual pattern in example 4.2) are subsequently detached and transposed to other melodic and harmonic contexts. They assume in this way a kind of life of their own, an independence that prefigures the serialization of rhythm (or duration) as a separate dimension in the works of Pierre Boulez, Milton Babbitt, and many others.

Of course, as we have noted, there were consequences to displacement. To allow the metrical displacement of a repeated chord to be felt by the listener, Stravinsky was obliged to hold to a strict beat when conducting his music, keeping expressive fluctuation (rubato) to a minimum. In due course, the strict performing style he favored became the rage among conductors and performers not only of contemporary music but of the classics as well. Stravinsky became known as an architect of the cool, detached manner ("playing it straight"), which in turn became identified with musical modernism. His neoclassical works were seen and heard in this light–as modernist, in other words–even if he himself always foreswore the label, doubtless because of its more widely recognized identification with the music of Schoenberg and his school. Stravinsky tended to underscore the diatonic/tonal, Baroque, and Classical origins of his middle-period music.

The expressive indications in the works of the late Romantics are worth recalling in this connection, markings that were applied no less liberally in the atonal and serial music of Schoenberg, Berg, and Webern. Even if radically new in pitch, the music of these latter composers was conceived in relation to the chromatic traditions of the 19th century. When Stravinsky made a study of this literature (Schoenberg, Berg, and Webern) during the 1950s, he ended up dismissing much of it; the expressive articulation, arising from the score or the performer alone, revealed a pathos or "emotional climate" that was overwrought and outdated. Even in Webern's music, much of which he extolled, the characteristic ritenutos and diminuendos became a source of irritation.

But the stiff, hardened surface of Stravinsky's music was never entirely a question of the metronomic beat and the role it served in highlighting rhythmic phenomena. No less of a contributing factor was the immediate repetition of motives and chords, often displaced metrically, but otherwise quite literal. The lack of variation lent the repetition a static and unyielding character, an air of intransigence. Especially early in the past century, with works such as *The Rite of Spring*, *The Wedding*, and the Piano Concerto, audiences were startled by these qualities. They seemed at odds with longstanding norms governing musical expression and expressivity.

Matching the severity of the composer's musical style was that of his religious values, the sort of God he worshipped (insistent and demanding), along with the rock-like inflexible nature of his beliefs. The Scriptures and the truths they conveyed were for a long while a daily calling for Stravinsky, a support system and undoubtedly the foundation of some of his frightening certainties about music and musical matters. Music and the character of his faith were linked in this fashion. The view of humankind and its prospects was a sober one.

Closely related to the strict, *non-espressivo* style were the composer's aesthetic beliefs, his ideas about the self-sufficiency of music, its inability or "powerlessness to express anything at all."[1] Later, in *Memories and Commentaries*, this notorious dictum was rephrased to read: "music expresses itself." The passions of music were specific to music, not a portrayal or *representation* of something outside of it. And it was only by virtue of their expression in music that the expressive qualities of music were expressive at all. Stravinsky was hardly the author of these formalist sentiments, but he was their most outspoken advocate among composers and performers of the past century.

If Stravinsky's contemporaries were relatively indifferent to his serial and 12-tone works of the 1950s and 60s, they were hardly so when it came to his Russian-period works. When, in the form of American minimalism, the inevitable revolt set in against the academies, serialism, and "difficult" music, it did so with the ostinatos, repetitive patterns, stratifications, polyrhythms, and metrical displacements of the earlier works in full view as a major point of departure. The minimalists were drawn to the static, repetitive, ritualistic, and impersonal qualities of this music. Even in one of Steve Reich's late works, *You are (Variations)* (2005), the ties to Stravinsky are unmistakable; specifically here, the sound of the four pianos in *The Wedding*, and the vocal style, staccato and heavily syncopated, in Stravinsky's *Symphony of Psalms*, third movement.

In the end, no doubt, experience transcends discourse. What counts most from the standpoint of the composer's legacy is the aesthetic charge of his music, the extent to which we, the listeners, are stirred by it. Much attention has been paid to the immediate response to music, the untranslatable nature of our attraction to one piece or another. Almost immediately upon impact, however, a form of reflection is likely to intervene, inflecting, and lending substance to what we hear. Unable to stay afloat indefinitely, attuned in rapturous self-forgetfulness, we are obliged to regroup in some fashion, to come to terms with experience. And we do so in an effort to sustain and further advance the immediate sense of rapport that would otherwise be lost. The hope of this book is that its discussion can work as an extension of this early reflective impulse and be of some concrete assistance to the listener. Such a purpose lay at the forefront of its conception.

Endnotes

Introduction

1. Fred Lerdahl, "Cognitive Constraints on Compositional Systems," in *Generative Processes in Music*, ed. John A. Sloboda (Oxford, Clarendon, 1988), 231-59.
2. See Taruskin (2016, 509).

Chapter 1

1. Walsh (1999).
2. Taruskin (1996, 86).

Chapter 2

1. See Taruskin (1996, 410).
2. See Cross (2015, 36-42).
3. Taruskin (1996, 537).
4. Sergei Grigoriev, *The Diaghilev Ballet, 1909-1929*, translated by Vera Bowen (London, 1953), 31.
5. Taruskin (1996, 588).

Chapter 3

1. See Walsh (1999, 144).
2. See Walsh (1999, 170).
3. Stravinsky and Craft (1962, 156).
4. Stravinsky and Craft (1960, 37).
5. See Walsh (1999, 195-96).

Chapter 4

1. Stravinsky and Craft (1962, 159).
2. Vera Stravinsky and Robert Craft, *Stravinsky in Pictures and Documents* (New York, 1978), 97-98.
3. Theodor W. Adorno, *Quasi una Fantasia: Essays on Modern Music*, translated by Rodney Livingstone (London, 1998), 151.
4. Matthew McDonald, "Jeux de Nombres: Automated Rhythm in The Rite of Spring, Journal of the American Musicological Society 63, 511.
5. David Huron, *Sweet Anticipation* (Cambridge, Mass.: 2006), 346-51.

Chapter 5

1. Constant Lambert, *Music Ho! A Study of Music in Decline* (London, 1966), 91.
2. Robert Craft and William Harkins, "Stravinsky's Svadebka (Les Noces)", *New York Review of Books* (14 December 1972), 23.
3. Stravinsky and Craft (1962, 101-03).
4. Stravinsky and Craft (1960, 98).
5. Arnold Schoenberg, *Style and Idea: Selected Writings of Arnold Schoenberg*, translated by Leo Black (Berkeley, 1985), 164-65.

Chapter 6

1. Stravinsky and Craft (1962, 136).
2. Stravinsky and Craft (1962, 138).

Chapter 7

1. Carr (2005), 3-4.
2. Ernest Ansermet. *L'Histoire de soldat,"* Chesterian 10 (Oct. 1920), 291.
3. Stravinsky and Craft (1963), 11.
4. Wilfrid Mellers, *Romanticism and the 20th Century* (New Jersey,

1957) 202.
5. Stravinsky and Craft (1969), 118.

Chapter 8

1. Stravinsky and Craft (1959), 11.
2. Stravinsky and Craft (1962), 114-16.
3. Stravinsky and Craft (1960), 108.
4. Robert Gjerdingen, "Meter as a Mode of Attending: A Network Simulation of Attentional Rhythmicity in Music", *Integral* 3, 67.

Chapter 9

1. Stravinsky and Craft (1959), 135.
2. Theodor W. Adorno, *Philosophy of Modern Music*, translated by Rodney Livingstone (London, 1996), 154.
3. H.G. Seashore "An Objective Analysis of Artistic Singing", in C.E. Seashore, ed., *Objective Analysis of Musical Performance* (Iowa City, 1937), 155.
4. Stravinsky (1947), 127.
5. Stravinsky and Craft (1962), 115.
6. Terry Eagleton, "Coruscating on Thin Ice," *London Review of Books* 30, no. 2 (2008), 19.

Chapter 10

1. Scott Messing, *Neoclassicism in Music from the Genesis of the Concept through the Schoenberg/Stravinsky Polemic* (Ann Arbor, 1988), 141.
2. Walsh (1999), 313.

Chapter 11

1. Stravinsky and Craft (1966), 42-44.

2. Walsh (1999, 173); Cross (2015), 112-14.
3. Stravinsky and Craft (1963), 71.
4. Taruskin (2016), 138.
5. Eric Walter White, *Stravinsky: The Composer and his Works* (Berkeley), (1966), 66.
6. See Taruskin (2016), 485-97.

Chapter 12

1. Stravinsky and Craft (1963), 11.
2. Walsh (1999), 484.
3. Stravinsky and Craft (1963), 11.

Chapter 13

1. See Taruskin (2016), 428-71.
2. Carr (2002), 2-9.
3. See Kimberly A. Francis, *Teaching Stravinsky; Nadia Boulanger and the Consecration of a Modernist Icon* (Oxford, 2015), 119.
4. Colin Slim, *Stravinsky in the Americas: Transatlantic Tours and Domestic Excursions from Wartime Los Angeles (1925-1945)*, from U Cal Press in January 2019.
5. Stravinsky and Craft (1962), 65-66.

Chapter 14

1. Robert Craft, "A Personal Preface", *Score*, no.20 (1957), 10.
2. Stravinsky and Craft (1969), 196. Pierre Souvtchinsky may well have been the author of this phrase.
3. Craft (2006), 171.
4. Stravinsky and Craft (1959), 79.
5. Stravinsky and Craft (1963), 76-78.
6. Fred Lerdahl, "Cognitive Constraints on Compositional Systems",

in *Generative Processes in Music*, ed. John A. Sloboda (Oxford, Clarendon, 1988), 231-59.

Chapter 15

1. *An Autobiography*, 35.

Suggested Reading

Robert Craft's *Chronicle of a Friendship* is a wonderfully detailed account of the Stravinsky-Craft partnership beginning in the late 1940s and ending with the composer's death in April of 1971. The later books by Craft, including *Down a Path of Wonder*, are no less instructive. Richard Taruskin's two-volume study, *Stravinsky and the Russian Traditions*, is brilliantly detailed, a major source where the composer's Russian-period works are concerned; Stephen Walsh's biography of the composer has become standard. And I can recommend three more recent books: Kimberly Francis's monograph on the Stravinsky-Nadia Boulanger friendship and collaboration in *Teaching Stravinsky*, Chandler Carter's wonderful study of *The Rake's Progress* in *The Last Opera*, and H. Colin Slim's *Stravinsky in the Americas*. My own books offer a more detailed discussion of melody, harmony, and rhythm in Stravinsky's music, topics that are surveyed in various chapters of this volume.

Carr, Maureen A. *Multiple Masks* (Nebraska, 2002).

—— ed., *Stravinsky's Histoire du soldat: A Facsimile of the Sketches*. (A-R Editions, 2005).

Carter, Chandler. *The Last Opera* (Indiana, 2019).

Craft, Robert. *Stravinsky: Chronicle of a Friendship* (New York, 1972).

_____ *Stravinsky: Glimpses of a Life* (New York, 1992).

_____ *Down a Path of Wonder* (2006).

Cross, Jonathan. *Igor Stravinsky* (London, 2015).

–––*The Stravinsky Legacy* (Cambridge, 1998).

Francis, Kimberly A. *Teaching Stravinsky; Nadia Boulanger and the Consecration of a Modernist Icon* (Oxford, 2015).

Horlacher, Gretchen. *Building Blocks: Repetition and Continuity in the Music of Stravinsky* (Oxford, 2011).

Neff, Severine, Maureen Carr, and Gretchen Horlacher, eds. *The Rite of Spring at 100* (Indiana, 2017).

Slim, H. Colin. *Stravinsky in the Americas: Transatlantic Tours and Domestic Excursions from Wartime Los Angeles (1925-1945)*, forthcoming from U Cal Press in January 2019.

Stravinsky, Igor. *An Autobiography* (New York, 1962). First Published in Paris, 1935.

_____ *Poetics of Music in Six Lessons*. Translated by Arthur Knodel and Ingolf Dahl. (Cambridge, Mass., 1947).

Stravinsky, Igor and Robert Craft. *Conversations with Stravinsky* (New York, 1959).

_____ *Memories an Commentaries* (New York, 1960).

_____ *Expositions and Developments* (New York, 1962).

_____ *Dialogues and a Diary* (New York, 1963).

_____*Themes and Episodes* (New York, 1966).

_____ *Retrospectives and Conclusions* (New York, 1969).

_____ *Themes and Conclusions* (New York, 1972).

Taruskin, Richard. *Stravinsky and the Russian Tradititons: A Biography of the Works through "Marva"* (Berkeley, 1996).

_____ *Defining Russia Musically* (Princeton, 1997).

_____ *Russian Music at Home and Abroad* (Berkeley, 2016).

Van den Toorn, Pieter C. *The Music of Igor Stravinsky* (New Haven, 1983).

_____ *Stravinsky and "The Rite of Spring"* (Berkeley, 1987).

Van den Toorn, Pieter C. and John McGinness. *Stravinsky and the Russian Period* (Cambridge, 2012).

Walsh, Stephen. *Igor Stravinsky: A Creative Spring. Russia and France, 1882-1934* (Berkeley, 1999).

_____ *Stravinsky: The Second Exile. France and America, 1934-1971* (New York, 2006).

About the Author

Pieter van den Toorn is Professor Emeritus of Music at the University of California, Santa Barbara, where he taught from 1990 to 2016. He is the author of *The Music of Igor Stravinsky* (1983), *Stravinsky and The Rite of Spring* (1987), *Music, Politics, and the Academy* (1995), and, with John McGinness, *Stravinsky and the Russian Period* (2012). Professor van den Toorn is a former student of the French musician and pedagogue Nadia Boulanger, for many years one of Stravinsky's closest colleagues and associates.

A Word from the Publisher

Thank you for reading *Simply Stravinsky*!

If you enjoyed reading it, we would be grateful if you could help others discover and enjoy it too.

Please review it with your favorite book provider such as Amazon, BN, Kobo, Apple Books, or Goodreads, among others.

Again, thank you for your support and we look forward to offering you more great reads.

www.ingramcontent.com/pod-product-compliance
Lightning Source LLC
Chambersburg PA
CBHW030151100526
44592CB00009B/222